FORERUNNERS: IDEAS FIRST FROM THE UNIVERSITY OF
MINNESOTA PRESS

Original e-works to spark new scholarship

FORERUNNERS: IDEAS FIRST is a thought-in-process series of
breakthrough digital works. Written between fresh ideas and fin-
ished books, Forerunners draws on scholarly work initiated in notable blogs, social media, conference plenaries, journal articles, and
the synergy of academic exchange. This is gray literature publish-
ing: where intense thinking, change, and speculation take place in
scholarship.

Clare Birchall
**Shareveillance: The Dangers of Openly Sharing and Covertly
Collecting Data**

Ian Bogost
The Geek's Chihuahua: Living with Apple

Andrew Culp
Dark Deleuze

Sohail Daulatzai
Fifty Years of "The Battle of Algiers": Past as Prologue

Grant Farred
Martin Heidegger Saved My Life

David Golumbia
The Politics of Bitcoin: Software as Right-Wing Extremism

Gary Hall
The Uberfication of the University

John Hartigan Jr.
Aesop's Anthropology: A Multispecies Approach

Mark Jarzombek
Digital Stockholm Syndrome in the Post-Ontological Age

Nicholas A. Knouf
How Noise Matters to Finance

la paperson
A Third University Is Possible

Akira Mizuta Lippit
Cinema without Reflection: Jacques Derrida's Echopoiesis and Narcissism Adrift

P. David Marshall
The Celebrity Persona Pandemic

Reinhold Martin
Mediators: Aesthetics, Politics, and the City

Shannon Mattern
Deep Mapping the Media City

Kelly Oliver
Carceral Humanitarianism: Logics of Refugee Detention

Davide Panagia
Ten Theses for an Aesthetics of Politics

Jussi Parikka
The Anthrobscene

Chuck Rybak
UW Struggle: When a State Attacks Its University

Steven Shaviro
No Speed Limit: Three Essays on Accelerationism

Sharon Sliwinski
Mandela's Dark Years: A Political Theory of Dreaming

UW Struggle

UW Struggle
When a State Attacks Its University

Chuck Rybak

University of Minnesota Press

MINNEAPOLIS

Published by the University of Minnesota Press, 2017
111 Third Avenue South, Suite 290
Minneapolis, MN 55401–2520
http://www.upress.umn.edu

The University of Minnesota is an equal-opportunity educator and employer.

Contents

Introduction	1
Real People	7
The Attack on Tenure	25
Failed Leadership	35
Eye on the Ball	45
No Confidence	63
Conclusion: Where Are We Now?	83
Acknowledgments	89

Introduction

There

When I was seventeen, I arrived at the SUNY Buffalo campus as a hopeful but underprepared student from a public high school with a violent reputation. My first attempt at the SAT resulted in a sub-1000 score. I had no idea what I wanted to study, what I cared for by way of a career, or what students did in an English department. SUNY Buffalo accepted me because they believed in Buffalo kids and in educating the people of their state. I received a Pell Grant and other need-based financial aid, or else I would not have been able to attend. Tuition was less than a thousand dollars.

Eventually I wandered into an English department and asked for directions from a disheveled man named Robert Creeley, who sent me to someone named Leslie Fiedler, who said I needed to go downstairs to find Carl Dennis and Susan Howe. All of these people were tenured, well-paid, supported state employees who set me on a path toward a meaningful life and career. Looking back now, this all feels like an accident, serendipity at its most immaculate.

But it was no accident. It was public education, exactly as designed by the generations before, waiting and working for me.

Public education completely saved and changed my life, and all I had to do was be alive and show up. I did not have "skin in the game" beyond my mother paying taxes (which should be skin enough). Nobody badgered me about "the needs of business" and "time to degree" or offered bizarre phrases like "from cradle to career." No one pushed me to work sixty hours a week and then take my education "at my own pace" while chained to a screen and fatigue. Public education cleared a space for me and allowed me to inhabit that area with all the glory of my imperfection.

I floundered for two years, righted my ship, and grew into the student who graduated with honors from the English program. Dr. Barbara Bono, mistress of Shakespeare, single-handedly made me believe in myself and that I could go on with my studies past a bachelor's degree. Again, I was allowed this just because I was there, as a breathing person, with interests. I had not yet earned anything.

I am not *that* old, but I can say I have achieved some positive accomplishment with my life (I hope to do more). I have taught in high school and higher education for more than twenty years. I can see results. Because teaching is a difficult profession, even just considering pedagogy alone, there were many growing pains along the way. But I have helped people. I have given back beyond the public's initial investment in providing me with opportunity.

Most of the effects of my public education are beyond assessment, and all of them came at minimal expense to the state. Public education, and public higher education, is not only a great achievement but also one of the most significant human achievements in recorded history. Across our nation and generations of citizens, versions of the story I have detailed here are too many to count.

Here

I now live in Green Bay and work at a four-year, comprehensive university that is part of the University of Wisconsin System. Although I was not born here, I consider my current life a homecoming: I work for a modest salary to help deliver public education to the state's citizens, many of whom are first-generation college students. My hope is that all my students will achieve success, personally and professionally, and that their education, a public good, will help them to advance and benefit our state and beyond in ways that show that the initial expense is a small investment with future rewards that exceed calculation. This, after all, is what I was privileged enough to have.

But to work for the state is not to agree with the state, and my conceptions of a shared common good are evaporating into illusion. I know now that there are no state university systems, only state legislatures. There are no laws, only lawmakers. The sooner we learn and accept this, the sooner we can go about fighting for and restoring one of America's most moral and vital institutions.

Currently, in Wisconsin, the state's legislature has traveled far down the road toward its destination of dismantling and reshaping public education—cuts in state support exceeded half a billion dollars in the last two budget cycles alone. Our legislature envisions an institution that no longer serves the state and its citizen students, instead opting for a corporatized agenda that caters entirely to the immediate "needs of business," a minimal curricular vision whose highest bar is "practicality" and "competence," and the whims of grudge-holding legislators who fear a well-educated electorate that might prioritize the long view and critical thought on any issue.

However, on the local level, we are easily caught up in distracting questions: why doesn't the University of Wisconsin

System president do something? Even with a half-million-dollar salary, he is both powerless and complicit, and complaining about his inaction is like complaining about the Queen of England. Why doesn't the state's Board of Regents do something? They are an extension of the legislature, appointed by a governor, Scott Walker, who once rescinded a student regent's appointment upon discovering he had signed a recall petition. Why don't individual chancellors stand and fight? They are also powerless, serving at the whim of the system president, who views all students, faculty, and staff as rhetorical pieces in the great lobbying chess match. In short, all views, proposals, and calls for action that exist outside of the state legislature are purely rhetorical and treated as such.

The sooner we realize this, the sooner we can focus our means on the appropriate, results-producing ends. The system president, faculty, staff, students: none of these people are to blame for state divestment in public higher education and concurrent attacks on academic freedom and job security. This has been legislated in Wisconsin, and if it has not already, all of this will soon be coming to your state: just ask Louisiana, Illinois, North Carolina, and Kansas, where, as I write this, institutions dedicated to public education are being shuttered.

The writing that follows is, in edited form, pulled from blog posts, written over a period of about two years, that chronicle the ongoing attacks on the UW System. As of July 2017, here is where we stand: staff have been laid off; faculty lines have been eliminated; UW-Madison's ranking as a research institution has fallen; faculty have seen their earned property right—tenure—rendered meaningless; shared governance has been eliminated and replaced with an "advise the CEO" model; faculty senates and staff across the system have voted "no confidence" in both the system president and the Board of Regents; and revenue projections continue to drop, feeding the bottomless and cruel maw of austerity. These are all features of our corporate conservative politics, not bugs.

Everywhere

What can recent events involving higher education in Wisconsin teach the nation? What can you, a reader in Ohio or Arizona, learn from the harbinger of the badger state? What can an attack on "the Wisconsin Idea" signal about the growing attacks on an American idea? The lessons are legion. In many ways, Scott Walker's Wisconsin has served as a laboratory for the nation's direction, and with the election of Donald Trump and the emergence of widespread one-party rule, the experiment is frothing to go national.

The first signs of this ideology's expansion have not been subtle. At the opening of 2017, both Iowa and Missouri drafted legislation proposing the elimination of tenure in their universities. Expect these trends to expand to a university near you. Anger alone will not stop the damage, and neither will protests, Facebook, or letters to editors. The only way to protect public higher education is by making it a relevant and focal political issue and voting appropriately. More importantly, people involved with public education must run for, and win, public office. This is the only road, because all roads lead to the legislature and policy.

This book provides a Wisconsin story that serves as a national warning. Supporting public education and its immense good is an easy thing to do. Let us try to remember the infinite rewards within our reach for what seems like such minimal effort and expense. If that is not practical, then I don't know what is. It is more than practical; it is miraculous.

Real People

AUSTERITY MEASURES, and the language promoting them ("flexibility," "efficiency," "accountability," "run like a business"), deliberately erase the human narratives affected by the actions of legislators and special interests—all of those terms essentially serve as a dehumanizing cover for firing people and treating them poorly. The following posts were an effort to remind readers that massive cuts to higher education would cost jobs, drive people away, and drain our local communities of vital citizens. This anti-intellectualism, disguised as "fiscal responsibility," is destabilizing quality public education across the country.

Real People

As I sit down to write this, I know it could be ten thousand words of sadness. I will limit myself.

Making news these days are the proposed buyouts University of Wisconsin campuses are offering to employees fifty-five and older; the buyouts are not automatic, as you must apply and be approved. But the buyouts are not a good deal, just as much of everything else is not a good deal. *The Green Bay Press Gazette* has a piece today[1] on buyout offers, and I know and work with the people quoted. Steve Meyer, one of the most respected and visible professors on our campus, said, "No way I am going to take them up on their offer. I am too far away from retirement to take it." He's right not to treat his career like a cheap suit; it is a sad offer among other sad offers. Also, the man is fifty-six. Fifty-six is young! (We can discuss ageism at another time.) Most importantly, if Steve did accept the offer, it would be a tremendous loss to our students, seeing the departure of yet another of our science faculty. This is a person we want to encourage to go away, even while fetishizing support for STEM fields?

But this isn't about buyouts. It is about our chronic hemorrhaging of talent. When you work at a campus like mine, UW–Green Bay, losing even *one person* to another job can be crippling; it often means, in some cases, that you are losing half or all of a popular program. I have heard people, and one legislator in particular, say that the "loss of talent" argument is not real. Make no mistake: the poachers are here. They have been here for years, as the post–Act 10 (or post collective bargaining) climate in Wisconsin has seen an increase in the departure of thriving, post-tenure professors.

The white noise hums, "We need you to be more like a business!" Is this what businesses do? Do successful businesses let their talent leave without so much as lifting a finger, all while the students dependent on that knowledge and skill stand by helplessly?

I want to make one point clear: this doesn't only matter in high-profile instances, such as those involving medical researchers.[2] It matters just as much on the smaller campuses,

1. http://www.greenbaypressgazette.com/story/news/education/2015/04/10/uwgb-staff-separation-offers/25609355/.

2. http://host.madison.com/wsj/news/local/education/university

in the teaching-and-learning trenches. Let me use my own campus as an example and name names; let me show you what we've lost and still stand to lose, and then apply this to your own circumstances and neighborhoods. Then let someone in the Wisconsin state legislature and UW Central show us that they care.

For some context, the undergraduate population at UW–Green Bay is largely female. Our most notable sports team is the women's basketball squad, annual powerhouse and future national champions. On our campus, it is vital that we have women in leadership, teaching, and administrative roles.

With that in mind, let me introduce you to Dr. Angela Bauer.[3] She is a biologist, a recognized teacher, and an expert in endocrinology and has demonstrated teaching excellence in both face-to-face and online environments. She chaired UW–Green Bay's biology department, and I'll shorthand this point by saying that a woman chairing a science department on our campus provides our students with an essential role model.

Here's another fact about Professor Bauer: she used to work at UW–Green Bay. She doesn't anymore.

Professor Bauer left in 2012 to become the chair of a biology department in North Carolina. We offered her almost nothing to stay. Our counter offer was an embarrassment. In the short time I worked with Dr. Bauer, what struck me most was how much she cared about teaching and how hard she worked at the craft. She rolled up her sleeves every day. She participated in teaching scholars projects to improve her students' learning. She was great at her job. She *is* great at her job, just not in Wisconsin.

/uw-madison-says-budget-uncertainty-cost-campus-two-top-medical /article_570bce8c-02ee-5cd7-ac03-af9799171ad2.html.

3. http://www.highpoint.edu/blog/2013/08/hpu-welcomes-new -biology-department-chair/.

Let me introduce you to Professor Aeron Haynie.[4] I had the pleasure of working alongside Professor Haynie in the English department at UW–Green Bay. She was a mentor to me, and on the occasions I observed her classroom teaching, I felt I was entering a robust, participatory environment where each student was deeply invested in her learning. Dr. Haynie's teaching knowledge, and performance, helped me to reinvent myself pedagogically. Dr. Haynie, because of her passion for teaching, took over UW–Green Bay's Center for the Advancement of Teaching and Learning and revitalized it. She also coedited an incredibly important book about teaching practice. At a time when the legislative gallery is calling for more and better teaching, Professor Haynie is *the* superlative example of this.

Here's another fact about Professor Haynie: she no longer works at UW–Green Bay.

In 2012 she received an unmatchable offer to direct the Center for Teaching Excellence at the University of New Mexico; it is unmatchable because, outside of Madison, the UW System lags significantly in competitive salaries. She left our teaching center, which we are likely downsizing because of the current budget travesty, to go to another university, where she trains teachers in the most important facet of their careers. Again, at a time when legislators incessantly harp about teaching, we let an actual teaching professional and scholar walk away. There are students on our campus who worked with Professor Haynie who still talk about her and lament her absence. We say teaching is important. We say we want more, more, more—we just don't want to pay for it. Is this how we behave "more like a business"?

4. http://news.unm.edu/news/haynie-named-director-of-the
-center-for-teaching-excellence.

Let me introduce you to Professor Kim Nielsen,[5] a history professor and expert in disability studies. In fact, she wrote *A Disability History of the United States*. What relevance could knowledge about disability have in contemporary work and technological environments? I wonder if there are people who are hired and paid very well to work in such areas. Professor Nielsen is, among other things, a full professor, a Fulbright Scholar, a National Endowment for the Humanities winner, and the author of five books.

Here's another fact about Professor Nielsen: she no longer works at UW–Green Bay.

Here is the last line of Professor Nielsen's current work bio: "She recently arrived at the University of Toledo after fourteen years at the University of Wisconsin–Green Bay." Yes, Professor Nielsen left in 2011, and as was the case in the other instances described, we did almost nothing to keep her here. We barely tried. The UW System had no use for her.

I've not even mentioned that we lost three members of our community. People who paid taxes, spent income, and contributed to the culture and fabric of the Green Bay area and of Wisconsin as a whole.

Keep in mind, these offers that out-of-state schools are making to UW faculty: they are overly generous when compared to the counter offers received. When you care about nothing but cuts, the UW is happy to shed talent; austerity cannot imagine another outcome. Another faculty member lost brings a sigh of relief from central offices, who can recoup the salary and fringe costs, and subsequently eliminate the faculty line, all while saying "no one lost a job!" Hardly. The people who lost the opportunity to apply for the vacant position lost that job.

5. https://www.utoledo.edu/llss/history/faculty/NielsenK.html.

The UW System is in trouble. It is, and has been, losing talent at a growing rate. I asked an administrator on our campus for figures and confirmed that the loss of tenured faculty is indeed on the rise. In her e-mail to me, she wrote, "Losing people post tenure is relatively rare and definitely seems to be trending upward." I have only mentioned three losses here but could extend this list to include at least fifteen others since 2011. I maintain a spreadsheet. Fifteen people in whom we invested significant time and funds. We are a small campus.

So what about today? What about for this coming year? The news gets worse.

Two tenured faculty members were just poached by a school in New York State. I know the details of the offer. If I told you what they are getting versus what they have now, you would gasp, laugh, then ask, "How do you keep anyone?"

One of the professors is in the arts and works in administration. She (we are losing another important female employee) is superior at her job, especially when connecting with the community. I'm sure New York will benefit from her work. The other is a communications professor who does important work in conflict resolution (who could possibly need such a skill?); he volunteered his services regularly at a conflict resolution center in Green Bay. I'm sure New York State will treat him well. Good-bye, Professors Mokren and Garcia—your students, colleagues, communities, and friends will miss you dearly.

Finally, there is Professor X. I'm not allowed to say anything specific about this because nothing is official. Professor X is my colleague. He is also about to be poached by a school that has had previous success in taking UW–Green Bay talent. Word gets around. Let me say a few words about Professor X: he's a national expert in his field; he's one of our campus's best and most popular teachers; his new book was just published; and he is irreplaceable in terms of teaching, research, and service to both the institution and the community. For what he is paid, he is an absolute bargain. If Professor X leaves, we will likely lose his position—a huge blow to our thriving department—because the position description doesn't include the words "engineering" or "business."

Let me state plainly the worst part of all this: Professor X wants to stay in Wisconsin. He told me this, even though the offer he has is yet another that makes you weep with how noncompetitive we are outside of Madison and business schools. Professor X said to me directly, "I'm looking for any reason to stay. Any counteroffer at all."

Our interim provost declined to make a counter offer. Nothing. Not ten dollars. In short, "just go." This is malpractice.

I could go on. Maybe about the female political science professor who left for a job in Ohio after her second year. Maybe I'll list the names of other people on the market or who have been contacted by head hunters. If I were an administrator in another state, here's the reality: I could offer almost any UW faculty member *a deal that is worse* than what the state's current faculty have but that would seem nothing short of heaven to the member of the UW. Poachers don't even have to try.

The pain doesn't end here.

It costs money to search for faculty. It also costs significant work hours. For example, I chaired a faculty search last year where I logged more than two hundred hours of work for not an extra cent of pay (shared governance is cheap, as *former* UW employee Sara Goldrick-Rab has explained[6]). So, in addition to the monetary costs of conducting a national/international search, which we are required to do, you are asking faculty/

6. http://www.jsonline.com/news/opinion/university-of
-wisconsin-system-needs-accountability-for-everyone-b99463142z1
-296507081.html.

staff to take on significant additional hours, for no additional pay, that draw them away from their more primary duties, like teaching. Yes, conducting searches is a welcome part of the job, until those searches become frequent and you find yourself searching for the same position twice in three years because you could not retain the original hire. High faculty turnover hurts the institution not only in terms of quality but also financially.

The following phrase is being uttered quite a bit in UW search meetings these days: "Do you think we can keep this person?"

All of this, added to the larger picture, has been devastating on morale. This is my fourteenth year in the University of Wisconsin System. I have never seen faculty and staff morale lower than it is now. People are working under significant mental strain, struggling to focus and perform while their jobs and worth are in question. Many have finally accepted that, as employees, our state-level bosses do not value us. When your value is under constant attack, doubt creeps into your own self-evaluation. This has mental and emotional effects. I'm not being dramatic when I say that tears have not been uncommon.

We are trying to buy people out of their contracts while we are losing people to other jobs. We are telling people of incredible value that they are no longer wanted or that we have nothing to offer to keep them.

Everything I've written here applies to the majority of UW System campuses. Our working conditions are the students' learning conditions, and the working conditions are crumbling.

The Long, Unnecessary Good-bye

This post continues the story introduced previously, where we learn the fate of one "Professor X."

Deliberate legislative and ideological malpractice is costing us friends, neighbors, colleagues, public servants, taxpayers, and the type of good, hardworking people everyone should support, regardless of political affiliation.

Below is a message sent yesterday by one of my colleagues at UW–Green Bay. This person is one of the most dedicated and respected people on our campus. As rumors have spread that this person might depart because of the toxic political climate, I have seen more than one student weep; others have expressed outrage that a mentor so important to them would be chased away from a university system that was once truly special. They say, "This can't be real."

Over the years, this colleague and I have had many students in common; I have seen, up close, the significant effect this colleague has had on their thinking, reading, writing, curiosity, engagement, confidence, expression, and overall personality. Frankly, there are students who cannot imagine their educations without this person. I understand why. I cannot imagine working in a space with such a glaring, self-inflicted void.

When talking about "star faculty" leaving the University of Wisconsin System, there are many misconceptions. Let me slay a few of those quickly and unequivocally:

"Star faculty" and staff do not congregate solely in Madison; they are abundant throughout the system. They are not rare in the UW; they are plentiful. Whereas schools like Madison, and maybe Milwaukee, have more at their disposal to retain such faculty and staff, the other comprehensive and two-year campuses do not. In many ways, campuses outside of Madison are more exposed because depleted resources neutralize viable counter offers. Poachers know this. They are here now, and "plentiful," the description I used above for high-quality faculty, may soon no longer apply. Amazing faculty and staff will remain, but the losses are deeply felt and negatively affect our mission and duty to our students.

"Well if they can get more money, they should go!" How naïve. To almost everyone I know in the UW, quality of life is far more important than salary: what is at stake here far exceeds economics. Our legislature is actively hostile to, and disparaging of, public employees, and the UW has been front and center of late. There are three other new departures to list from my campus—in all cases, it is more than money and job security that are the cause; the open hostility of our state's leadership is a more significant factor than ever. More than one faculty/staff member has said to me, "I just can't stay where I'm despised. I can't have my children hear people talk about me this way." I get it. I have two daughters. It's a surreal moment when your eight-year-old asks, "Why does Governor Walker hate schools and teachers so much?"

So here is the letter. They are a real person's words, experience, and pain. To hear them is to hurt, especially given how easily all of this could have been avoided via governance that didn't prioritize grudges and division.

Dear Colleagues,

Most of you know that this e-mail has been a long time coming, but that hasn't made it any easier to write. It's been something of an open secret for a while that I've been offered the position of Chair of English at High Point University, and I'm writing to let all of you know that I've accepted that position. I will be submitting my letter of resignation from UW–Green Bay later this week, and I'll be moving to North Carolina in August.

When I came to Green Bay thirteen years ago, I never dreamed I would ever leave. Wisconsin has been and always will be home to me. School and jobs have taken me away several times, but I've always seemed to end up back here. I've done the math, and it turns out that I've lived thirty-four of my forty-four years in this state. Before the passage of Act 10, there was no way on earth I would ever have considered applying for another job. This year I applied for jobs mostly to hedge my bets against possible disaster, and as you all know, since I applied, that disaster has arrived. As a proud graduate of the system's flagship institution, this was and is the ideal job for me, but it has become very difficult to watch the dismantling of the system and the state that I love, especially since my livelihood depends on them. Those of you who know me best know how incredibly painful it is for both me and my family to leave, but I simply cannot afford to deprive myself and my family of this opportunity for a brighter future.

Over the past couple months, I've winced as people in my position have been described as "defectors." That description is appropriate in one sense, since what we are now engaged in is nothing less than a war for the future of public higher education (and particularly the kind we in the humanities and the liberal arts value) in this state. I hope all of you will realize that although I am leaving the system and the state, I am no defector in that war: I am on no side but yours. While even a pessimist like me can see that the political climate in Wisconsin is bound to change for the better sometime soon, I'm afraid that some of the changes that are being made to what we all do for a living are irreversible. The only thing that encourages me is that I know what capable and determined advocates remain among UW faculty to fight to mitigate the damage, all of you among them.

I cannot imagine ever working with a better group of colleagues than I have had the pleasure to work with in my thirteen years at UW–Green Bay. I admire you all enormously, and I am honored to call all of you both my colleagues and my friends. Given its size and its incredibly diverse faculty, [the Humanistic Studies Department] should never have worked, but in the time I've been here it has worked spectacularly. In fact, it is the most functional department I have ever been in or around. That is due largely to the almost miraculously collegial atmosphere we've managed to establish. And the unique interdisciplinary education in the humanities that we have managed to provide for our students is something to be proud of and very much worth fighting for. Even though the prospect of living in Wisconsin helped to entice me, the most important reason I came here was the opportunity to work in such an environment. I desperately hope you can manage to preserve it in some form.

Although I am leaving, I plan to be a frequent visitor, at least in the coming year. I hope I will get a chance to see all of you at some point during those trips. In the meantime, please know that I wish nothing but the best for all of you and for this institution. In this case, the cliché that the decision to leave was the hardest one I've ever had to make happens to be true. The way my life has gone, the chances seem pretty good that I'll be back someday. I know you'll all do your best to save this place while I'm gone.

Best,

Bryan Vescio

There it is. Good-bye to a neighbor, a taxpayer, a homeowner, a consumer, a Wisconsin vacationer, and a wonderful family. Why would we want any of those living in Wisconsin, and specifically Green Bay?

I will also add this: the constant bullying of this state of its own employees is going to separate this family for a year.

My soon-to-be ex-colleague will move on alone for the year to the new job, while the remainder of the family stays so their children can finish school. Think about that. We are talking about a person who has given a significant portion of his life to do outstanding work for this state; a person who just earned the distinguished rank of full professor at a pay rate that stands at half of what might be earned somewhere else; a person who wanted to stay here and looked for any reason at all to do so. How did the legislature respond? *Your accomplishments mean nothing, and we are now going to make the tenure status you earned meaningless. Have fun spending a year away from your family.*

How can Wisconsinites stand by and watch their neighbors be treated so shabbily? My colleague didn't. As an educator, this person helped Wisconsin citizens, many of them first-generation college students, advance in their lives and move beyond any barriers that held them back. Students who worked with this person knew they were valued; they were respected.

The state and our central administration could not return the basic courtesy.

What's Old Is New

As our state legislature, in cooperation with our Board of Regents and system president, dismantle the earned property right in the form of tenure protections, explicitly for the purpose of laying off tenured faculty, there has of course been no move to lessen the workload required by the tenure process. In fact, the opposite is happening: as pay, benefits, and earned job security decrease, faculty responsibility increases under the austerity slogan "do more with less." While UW faculty must dedicate years of their lives and work to earning tenure, it can now all be wiped away at a whim, hence the broad reasoning of "program discontinuance, curtailment, modification, or redirection." I have a front row seat to this in a way that exceeds my own experience, as my wife and I are professors in the same department. This piece is a reflection on the day my wife began the process of "going up" for the rank of full professor.

As I sit down to write this quick post, my wife is driving to her unit-level review for the rank of full professor. This meeting should be entirely celebratory. The gods and heroes demand it.

As someone who has seen her entire career unfold up close, I can say with ample support that the UW is lucky to have her, our campus is lucky to have her, and she has worked tirelessly for fifteen years to get to this point. Yes, if she worked in a different state at a different campus she would make 20K more per year (which adds up to about 300K in lost revenue and counting), but UW–Green Bay is a special place. This is not hyperbole. The students, staff, faculty, and alumni are a treasure.

I consider myself lucky to work there as well, not because "I'm just happy to have a job" but because of the place and spirit and intention that extends all the way back to the university's founding by a bunch of crazy people with a crazy dream.

She's probably just driving over the Leo Frigo Bridge right now, and her meeting begins in ten minutes. And so my message to the Board of Regents, Wisconsin legislators, and UW Central and President Ray Cross is, I wish that she could walk into this moment of tremendous accomplishment and leave with more than self-satisfaction.

You see, what she is going through today is essentially post-tenure review (that thing that legislators pretend doesn't exist)—that's what the march from assistant to associate to full professor is: another lengthy, regular demonstration of superlative accomplishment. So why do the Board of Regents and legislators keep saying that post-tenure review is something we don't have but desperately need? Hint: The goal is not really post-tenure review. The goal is an overdetermined process for shedding salary costs.

As my wife is surely pulling in to the campus parking lot at this point (she tends to run late, or at least cut close all her travels—she stole my coffee as she was leaving), let me point to a few other things my wife (and others) have had to do since receiving tenure: I have watched her put hours into gathering documents for merit reviews knowing full well there was no money to reward that merit. Tell me again how we want to reward high performers. Tell me again how good "résumé-based" systems of application are: my wife has résumé for days, yet, outside of her campus, has been repeatedly told that her most important ability is her ability to be fired. Sound familiar? This is Wisconsin. This is America.

So, Board of Regents, President Cross, skeptical legislators, I am not convinced that you care, but let me give you a look into accomplishment as we hit 8:59 and the committee in the meeting room is saying hello, maybe commenting on today's glum weather, and hopefully drinking coffee from steaming mugs. For all the false complaints that achieving tenure leads to poor performance, my wife gave birth to both of our children *after* she was tenured. She only got better at her job. I watched her pump breast milk in her office while preparing for class. I watched her win the campus's most prestigious teaching award on virtually no sleep. I watched her struggle with the realization that minimum sixty-hour workweeks take her away from her family. I watched her build a nationally recognized, student-run arts journal with her own hands while simultaneously providing students with important training for the workforce (ask them; they'll tell you). I've watched her develop new curriculum over and over and over. Her area of specialty is now the most popular emphasis in our department. Just yesterday, a successful young professional returned to the UW–Green Bay campus to give a presentation to our students. Not only was the presentation inspiring and a huge success but I'll take a moment to point out that my wife played an instrumental role in this person's march toward a career. That's what she does. Every day. That's what we do in the UW as public servants. Every day.

It's 9:15. In a room somewhere on campus a group of highly accomplished people are celebrating my wife's accomplishments. None of those people are regents, a system president, or legislators.

Stop the circus and the smoke. There is no hollower word in our vocabulary today than "advisory." Our budget debacle and subsequent actions are sincerity's discarded husk. None of this is about quality, about rewarding performance, and insert other platitudes here. It's about shedding people, bringing them lower, regardless of rank and accomplishment. It's about the sickening glee taken in the mere idea of shuttering programs and campuses, and when you hear talk of such plans already moving into the open, it's clear that tenure "reformation" is nothing but deformation. The point is not to reward performance; the point is to ignore it. Stop pretending that there's disagreement about what tenure is, or that this is all about an update that "brings us into line" with peers just as unmoored as we are now. When lost, dead reckonings take skill and courage.

It would be nice if my wife (9:22 now—they are surely carrying her around the room in the fashion of a Roman triumph) could accept all of this as more than a personal accomplishment. Shock: *professional accomplishments are supposed to be professional.* The state of Wisconsin is her boss, so treat her as a professional and reward her for her work. It would be nice if this peak, arrived at after over twenty years of study, training, and work, could be realized in a rank with actual meaning rather than wiped away in the great leveling that is so obvious to everyone with skin. You can say a lot of things about UW faculty and staff regarding issues like tenure, but I know this—at least we're honest about it.

It's 9:40. Obviously, the meeting is still going on. They will need until at least noon to cover a mere micron of her body of work. (A bard is plucking strings, moving through the epic lineage.)

President Cross, you should call her in her office and congratulate her later. (Even though this meeting today is only the first step.) After all, current post-tenure review exceeds the boundaries of one meeting or layer of approval. If anything, we are an overdetermined bunch already. She would like to hear from you. I like to think the best of people, so I'm opening myself to the possibility that all support and encouragement must be kept inside, spoken in private, so as not to antagonize testy legislators. I get it. In this case, no one else will be listening. Knowing my wife like I do, any praise or words of encouragement will be appreciated.

My wife would never write something like I'm writing now (9:50: they are feeding her grapes and preparing a hecatomb)— she has too much class. I, however, have no class, so let me point out one big difference between my wife and the assembled group of people who are drafting policy to render her accomplishments meaningless beyond personal satisfaction:

She can do your jobs; you can't do hers.

The Attack on Tenure

ALTHOUGH THE REAL EDUCATION CRISIS IN WISCONSIN is entirely legislative and budget related, you wouldn't know this. One of the most reliable strategies employed by journalists, paid editorialists, think tankers, legislators, regents, and even our own system president is to make faculty always appear to be the focus of the problem. Wisconsin is in a budget crisis, not a faculty crisis or tenure crisis or mythical "skills gap" crisis. You wouldn't know that if you followed the in-state coverage of the UW saga—this performance requires that faculty always be the problem, no matter how powerless of a constituency they truly are. This piece is one of many that speaks to this scapegoating.

Tenured Kingpins

When debating higher education reform, a clear indicator that genuine economic concerns are a smokescreen for misinformed ideological ones[1] is how fast the word "tenure" emerges

1. http://www.jsonline.com/news/education/professors-group -raises-red-flag-on-scott-walkers-uw-system-plans-b99461011z1 -296085811.html.

in the discussion. For anyone with even basic knowledge of the higher-ed landscape, tenure is about the ten-thousandth item on the list of "problems," and even then, the problem is not tenure's existence but its contraction for the purposes of labor exploitation.

As this Scylla is again trying to steer us toward Charybdis, here is a fact sheet I am now posting for the fourth time. I hope this comes in handy if you once again find yourself besieged by Captain Taxpayer, Mr. Business, Harvey VandenFreedom, or FaceTwitter SuperTroll.

TENURE FACT SHEET

- Percentage of tenured faculty who currently govern the state in which they work: 0%
- Percentage of active tenured faculty who serve as the system president: 0%
- Percentage of tenured faculty who work as faculty while also serving as the chancellor of their institution: 0%
- Percentage of tenured faculty who serve on boards of regents: 0%
- Percentage of tenured faculty who are asked to contribute their wisdom to the process of what tuition will be: 0%
- Percentage of tenured faculty who give themselves raises: 0%
- Percentage of tenured faculty who, in their abundant free time, currently serve in state legislative bodies: 0%
- Percentage of tenured faculty who, as legislators, voted to cut the budget of the institutions where they work: 0%
- Percentage of tenured faculty who can single-handedly reform state Medicaid costs to free up money for higher education: 0%
- Percentage of tenured faculty who refused to accept federal dollars for health care reform: 0%
- Percentage of tenured faculty who manage and write the state budget: 0%

- Percentage of tenured faculty who assign tax breaks to businesses and individuals: 0%
- Percentage of tenured faculty who turned a projected surplus into a significant budget shortfall: 0%
- Percentage of tenured faculty who are responsible, in any way, for Wisconsin's current budget crisis: 0%
- Percentage of tenured faculty who opt to hire expensive consultants instead of using in-house expertise: 0%

More Fun Facts

As current data from the U.S. Department of Education[2] show, as do several other sources, institutions of higher ed are opting for labor exploitation over job security, thus aligning its practice with, well, the globe: in 2011, full-time tenured faculty composed just over 15 percent of instructional staff, down from nearly 30 percent in 1975. So damn that tenured class for . . . shrinking significantly?

The primary culprit for rising costs is a combination of state divestment and a boom in administrative hiring. Given that, it's not hard to see why someone in the legislature might want to distract from the fact that he champions his "tuition freeze" to mask that state support has dropped over 20 percent in a mere six years,[3] which has then led to tuition increases that exceeded 20 percent.

Surely the tenured kingpin is to blame!

And finally, our central administrators occasionally collaborate in this misconception, and the declining ratio of faculty

2. http://chuckrybak.com/wp-content/uploads/2015/03/AAUP_Trends_In_Professor_Employment.jpg.
3. http://chuckrybak.com/wp-content/uploads/2015/03/State-Percentage.png.

members per administrator[4] might have something to do with it. According to the Delta Cost Project, in 1990, public research universities had 3.2 faculty/staff positions for every executive/professional staff member; as of 2012, that number had declined to 2.2. At institutions like mine (public bachelor's colleges), in 1990, that ratio was 4.3 to 1. In 2012, it had declined to 2.5 to 1. Faculty are not the cause of rising costs.

Thanks for listening! Always remember, faculty, who control everything, are also to blame for everything. Be the tenured kingpin you are!

Moses in Bullet Points

The UW saga has made abundantly clear the inadequacy of our centralized leadership model, which prioritizes UW-Madison and the lobbyist/legislative class over the local communities who most rely on the system and who understand its very specific contributions to local communities and economies. This post is one that begins detailing the ineffectiveness of our current model.

We live in a leadership void. And although it is tempting to wax furious on larger levels (the U.S. Senate just voted on whether climate change is "real"), I'll keep my focus on our capsizing state and its university system.

What is there to say about this drama? Is it a comedy? A tragedy? I'm more inclined to interpret it as performance art about irony. For example, it is amazing to watch people participate in an entirely linguistic process while simultaneously questioning

---

4. http://chuckrybak.com/wp-content/uploads/2015/03/05
-Delta-Cost-daily.gif.

the value of the humanities. It is amazing to watch "Americans for Freedom and Up-Pulled Bootstraps" fetishize authority to the point that words like "boss" and "CEO" feel like catalysts for arousal.

Enter our hero and savior: "flexibility." As we know, "flexibility" is austerian code for cutting pay, benefits, and jobs. Speaking of performance art . . .

Here's a question I ask myself every day: why would anyone sitting in our legislature listen to system president Ray Cross? This is not a criticism of Cross (he could be Ronald Reagan) but ultimately a question about meaningful and representational organizational structure. What can antagonistic legislators possibly be thinking when meeting with President Cross beyond, "Oh great, here's the guy begging for money again! This is so boring. What can we do for fun and liven this up? Make him squirm!"

Here are some choice quotes from Cross's recent Q&A at UW-Whitewater:[5]

- On tenure and promotion: "The current concern by legislators at the Capitol focuses on this single issue—you should not have a guaranteed job for life; that is the sound bite logic that is being played," he said. "Let's break that down. When you tell the legislators that they really don't have it like that, they do not see that. They ask, 'Well, how many tenured faculty have been let go?' The answer is very few. Then you explain the process of securing tenure, how you get there and the probation process. There has been all kinds of scrutiny and screening before tenure is awarded." (Note: none of this has anything to do with the budget shortfall, which is the fault of legislators, who, of course, make the budgets. This is

5. http://www.dailyunion.com/news/article_841cc5c6-f006-11e4 -976c-bb6cba9a88bd.html.

a nonmonetary issue. Why is this even a point of discussion? Because faculty must always be front and center to serve as rhetorical punching bags.)

- On "job creators" fetishizing the ability to fire people: "Cross said some legislators understand the process, yet still say that some faculty should be dismissed due to performance." (Note: why are faculty, again, the front-and-center topic of discussion for a budget shortfall and cut they have nothing to do with? Why aren't the budget makers front and center? Leadership! See my previously posted "Tenure Fact Sheet.")

- On legislators' incessant fetishizing of authority and submissive workers: "Number one is that 'employees should not get to pick their boss,'" he said. "They believe the policy we have for hiring chancellors or executives, which requires a majority of the search committee be composed of faculty, is offensive. That is easy to fix. That is a board policy, not a statute." (Think about this for a moment, and take note parents and students: your education is meant to teach you submission. In short, why does the UW promote such an "offensive" democratic system?)

- On the fog of war that many legislators exist in: "Some legislators say that faculty and student input needs to be advisory," Cross said. "I open to 36.09 and say 'show me where it is not advisory—because it is advisory.' I think there is a lack of understanding about what shared governance is and where it needs to go. Part of our job is to help legislators understand that." (President Cross states the reality: shared governance has always been a performance more akin to playing house. Also, we need to prioritize businesses, which often pay no state taxes, over students, who pay both state taxes and tuition. Check.)

Doesn't all of this seem so pointless? Is there anything here that speaks to education, aspirations, access, or opportunity? Can you remember the last time anyone asked or cared about what students want? The preceding items dominate the write-up of the Q&A. None of them are budget related. *Zero*. Is the cut about a real shortfall or about the UW's "behavior"? It can't be both. We live in a leadership vacuum where governance is by petty grudge. Let us ask ourselves a few questions:

- What do you say to a leader/legislator who says we have too many campuses, too many departments, too many everything, while that same person spent most of the last year arguing that we needed a third Walmart inside a ten-mile radius in sprawling Green Bay?

- How do you engage leaders/legislators who embrace the imaginary vision that faculty have power in the contemporary, corporatized university? How do you talk about education in the face of frothing misconception? To an audience that offers nothing beyond, "But the faculty! Why can't we fire them or at least micromanage them to death because . . . leadership! Accountability!"

- How to you dispel the myth of "we need to do a better job of communicating who we are" when the root of the word "university" should successfully convey the impossibility of such a definition. I've worked in the UW for thirteen years; even now I'd consider my understanding of "what we do" to be minimal. There is *so much* going on at one time on any given campus, let alone in the system as a whole, that any definition is simplistic and a disservice. Furthermore, why emphasize the need for a single person to be able to "understand the system"? Good luck, and again, I say that as an insider without such an understanding. Knowledge is an essential economy, whether that economy is financial, cultural, local, global, personal, emotional, artistic, or educational.

- How do you reach a leader/legislator who boasts of protecting the middle class from tuition hikes while simultaneously voting for Act 10 and Right to Work legislation and is currently pushing the repeal of prevailing wage laws?

- How do you expect leadership to function in the present when legislators refer to the guiding wisdom and data-driven "bad taste in the mouth" rule from a previous non-troversy? (This refers to the fact that UW campuses kept reserve funds on hand for difficult times. Although this is common "like a business" practice, the legislature acted un-aware.)

- How do you persuade anyone who views knowledge en-tirely as a vocational subset of work and consumerism? We are broadcasting to students and parents of students every-where, "Come to us for knowledge so you can be silenced under the all-important boss." Great. Exactly what I want for my daughters.

- How do we inhabit a space where traditional and rigid top-down leadership bludgeons their constituents with talk of "change," "flexibility," and "being open to new ideas"? (That's irony over there in the coffin, stake through the heart.)

- What do you say to leadership that rambles on about quality while that very quality is running out of the door?[6]

- What do you say to leadership that offers quotes from David Brooks and Thomas Friedman in place of ideas anchored in our real, lived experience? What do you say to this leader-ship that prioritizes external ideas over internal talent and resources?

- What kind of leadership anchors its decisions on the latest Rebecca Blank (the Madison chancellor) quote or the latest faculty comment? "Oh, we were concerned about education in Wisconsin, but forget it now, Rebecca Blank said some-thing!" Good lord.

- Lastly, why do we pretend that a leader/system president can effectively speak with this leading, ideological class when those legislators have no incentive to listen? This is not about President Cross—it is independent of the person who holds that position—but in what scenario is this model even remotely effective rhetorically?

6. http://chuckrybak.com/uw-struggle-real-people-edition/.

This is what a leadership vacuum sounds like. Who knew there could be so much noise in a vacuum?

Throughout this year, a year filled with despair, I've learned and been reminded of some important things that I believe connect to leadership.

First, the students are the true owners of this university system because they provide the largest portion of its funding via tuition dollars. They are also silenced in proportion to their contribution, and it is no wonder that some legislators are upset that students would want a say in the enterprise they significantly fund. Again, students are the majority stakeholder in an organization that provides them with the least power. Can students sue for control of the system? They deserve it. On my campus I've watched students bravely organize, protest, and communicate with legislators in a way that I can confidently say puts UW Central's leadership to shame. These students, with so much at stake, have decided to mobilize, to "fight," with their intelligence and passion. Furthermore, when they meet face-to-face with legislators, they stand there as something that UW Central never does: voters. In that moment, legislators cannot simply roll their eyes without some risk. Our system is on the verge of not deserving the wonderful students we serve.

Second, though Ray Cross likes to ask, "How do you think they got that way?" when referencing legislators who want to help the UW, my belief is that the communication from students, parents, community leaders, business leaders, staff, and faculty has had far more of an influence on this process than it is given credit for. Though dispersed and collaborative, it sure looks a lot like real leadership. And I hope that with a 2016 presidential election on the way, the UW remains a state-level ballot-box issue regardless of our bleak budget outcome. These efforts must not be wasted and must make their way into the language of upcoming campaigns for office. Dear students, parents of students, staff, faculty, alumni . . . consider running.

I've talked around the elephant in the room: our governor is the model for our leadership vacuum. No decision is about Wisconsin or its citizens anymore. We know this. We are a laboratory for hourly polling services. The UW is drowning in a fiction of flexibilities, efficiencies, nimbleness, and the twenty-first-century global something or other. But the UW is people. Until we have leaders who acknowledge people as people, every meeting, town hall, press release, "listening" session, is nothing but performance.

The leadership vacuum presents itself when all discussion is about everything but the problem of state government, instead focusing on the red herrings of faculty, tenure, governance, some legislator's bad taste in the mouth, or cash reserves. The problem is not the UW. The problem is the inadequate budget and the architects of our current budget shortfall. If we prize accountability so much, we should then hold the legislature accountable for the budget they created and voted for. To do that, of course, we need accurate information. There is nothing else to talk about. It's hard to control this outside of our own organization, so I wish UW leadership would embrace this reality instead of indulging the fiction that somehow the composition of search committees is important.

How long can I ramble on about all this nontalk about nonissues? The question should not be, How do we do better next time? Going forward, our many questions should begin with, How can we change the UW's leadership model to one where our voices actually have meaning?

Failed Leadership

THERE ARE MANY CONSTITUENCIES who deserve criticism for what is happening to the UW System, and the system president, Ray Cross, is no exception. In times of austerity, visionaries take a backseat to bureaucrats and their short-term, mechanical goals. The territory of dreamers is colonized by middle-grade ideologues. This is the case with many institutions of higher education across the country, including the UW System. Instead of talking about our moon shots, about curing disease and producing tomorrow's leaders, we brag about "streamlining back-office operations" or being a "pipeline" to cubicles in need of an occupant (why do people use "pipeline" as a positive metaphor?). When you have a lobbyist instead of a leader, everyone outside of power is a rhetorical piece ready to be sacrificed again and again to please legislators for whom nothing is ever enough.

Final Update

Austerity is the death of the imagination. The death of ideas and their very possibility. And thus the only line of the current UW "budget" plan I need quote is this:

38. Shared governance, general: Specify that, with regard to the responsibilities of the faculty, academic staff, and students of each institution, "subject to" means "subordinate to."

This has always been about faculty. The level of obsession with faculty, with bringing talented, humble, and hardworking people to heel—the people most responsible for delivering the university's mission—approaches pathology.

President Cross, the Board of Regents, and a hostile legislature collaborated to more fully extend Act 10 to the public university system, and they can barely contain their glee. When Regent President Falbo refers to "a new tone" for the UW, he means "shut up faculty." Falbo, like the legislature, fetishizes authority; their imaginations cannot extend beyond the conceptual framework of "the boss." They cannot imagine democracy. The central purpose of the omnibus bill is to clear the way to fire faculty, at will, with no effort required for cause—our austerian overlords must simply cite program "discontinuance, curtailment, modification, or redirection." What doesn't count as modification or redirection? Given the preceding language, it's hard to come up with a condition where faculty *cannot* be fired.

And like Wisconsin's K–12 teachers, who can be fired based solely on *budget projections* or anticipated shortfalls, the same tactic will be applied to UW faculty. We have already seen cuts based on a budget that does not yet legally exist. Expect projected cuts and shortfalls to provide future justifications for firing faculty. The bill's language anchors upon economic causes for dismissal, but that's merely the garb retribution dons these days. Last year, I sat in a K–12 school board meeting where the members and superintendent explained: *if there is a projected budget shortfall, we can fire you, but when the money comes through late in the process, we can rehire you, or someone else, back at a starting salary.* These are human beings, talking about other human beings.

And so what's left for me to update or blog about? What difference has any of it made? Let me take a detour into the personal. Forgive me for this; I've always tried not to do that here.

I started in the UW in 2003, working for the UW Colleges. My then-to-be wife was hired into the UW the previous year, and after a year apart, I moved to Wisconsin expecting to teach high school (which I had been doing in Ohio while finishing my dissertation). But I got lucky: my degree plus my tech skills secured my job at UW–Washington County, where I was the first person hired by the UW Colleges with online teaching built into his contract.

We live in Green Bay. Washington County is a hundred miles away from Green Bay. So for six years I commuted just under two hours each way. I lost hundreds of family, work, and creative hours sitting in my car. But I was deeply happy, and I loved and believed in Wisconsin. I started my career here. My first year in Wisconsin, I married my wife (with apparently great symbolism, the ceremony was on a cliff's edge at Cave Point in Door County), then we bought our first and only home, and soon both of our daughters were born. The most important moments of my personal and professional life are Wisconsin. I am from Buffalo, but Wisconsin is my home.

Pregnant with our second daughter, my wife was in a car accident. Our one-year-old was in the car as well. I didn't know about it. I was teaching classes more than a hundred miles away. A staff member finally alerted me, and I made yet another bad-weather drive, at great speed, up Highway 41 to a Green Bay hospital. I couldn't reach her or speak with her, or even know what was happening. She was, as required, out of reach and hooked up to a fetal heart monitor. Everything turned out fine, except the blunt realization that I had to change jobs. I couldn't be that far away.

Again, I got lucky. A job opened at UW–Green Bay in my fields of expertise. For my family, I gave up my hard-earned tenure and accepted the job. It took me two weeks to decide, as I'd be giving up tenure in the climate of a newly passed Act 10. But I earned tenure again. I've earned tenure in the UW System twice. I am aware of luck; I am aware of fortune and circumstance; but I'm also aware that, postluck, I worked and worked and worked and earned my rank. In my first seven years I worked no less than eighty hours a week with a 4/4 teaching load (which was one-fourth of my overall *workload* and appointment responsibility). I have dedicated my entire professional life to helping people make their lives better. Nothing makes me happier than when my students are hired into the workforce at salaries that exceed my own. Nothing makes me happier than a returning student rediscovering a passion for writing that also leads to the student receiving a promotion and a raise. As a professional and state employee, I work and live and breathe for others. Yet, last night, my wife and I found ourselves asking, "Why does this state hate us so much? What have we done wrong?"

And that's my question for President Cross, who, upon securing expanded authority for himself and the Board of Regents, is moving swiftly to curtail the job security of UW employees: why do you have such disdain for what people have worked tirelessly to earn?

And for the legislature that barks incessantly about work, about earning your way, about not "freeloading": why do you dismiss my work and accomplishments? Why look at a class of people who do so much right as if they are always what is wrong? These questions are rhetorical.

So again to President Cross, legislators, regents, and the people reveling in an imagined comeuppance: how are teachers supposed to face students and encourage them to work toward goals and achievements? Are we to lie and say the work will pay off when the fruits of our own labor are constantly derided, devalued, and destroyed? That question is not rhetorical. What should we tell students to work toward? Maybe we should listen to Regent Falbo and simply offer, "Find your bosses. They'll tell you what you're worth."

I feel this needs repeating, and consider this portion an open letter: President Cross, Regent Michael Falbo, Senator Alberta Darling, Speaker Robin Vos, other republican legislators—why do I, and people like me, not deserve what we earned? Why is our work not valuable? Why did the state and the UW ask us to go through this grueling process only to back out on its end of the commitment? It is so contrary to what you offer in public statements and speeches.

Let me put this another way, and again, forgive me for the personal tone and reference: tenure is not a perk for me. I did not erroneously stumble into tenure. It was not "awarded." I earned it. Twice. But more importantly, it is a symbol of my work, skill, and accomplishment. In my professional life, tenure is a source of pride not because I get to sleep on a state yacht but because it signifies nearly *two decades* of my life: the study, training, job searches, students and their triumphs, individual and book publications, teaching awards, community work, institutional work, and so on. Twenty years of my life and dedication, wiped away with a grudge and a brushstroke. I'm demoralized and, like many of us, wondering, *What was all the work for?* In short, the only people who have done their jobs, who lived up to the promise of the UW, are faculty and staff. This is how we are rewarded. President Cross has said he and the regents will "reinstitute" tenure. Maybe in name, but not in any form that fulfills the promise and commitments made to us upon being hired. This is betrayal, and it hurts. It has taken its toll on me, my mental health, my ability to focus on my job, my relationships. Have I failed in some way? President Cross, Robin Vos, Alberta Darling, I sincerely ask, where did I go wrong?

So I'll leave with this, for all of my colleagues and compatriots in the UW—faculty, staff, students, two deans I can think of—I am so honored to be one of you. Maybe everyone has a little bit of impostor syndrome, and not a day goes by that my breath is not taken away by the sheer amount of intelligence, dedication, self-sacrifice, backbone, and curiosity that surround me. Such goodness, such people, here in a darkening Wisconsin, is a blessing. It is not your fault that our state and our UW leadership have abandoned imagination as a resource.

Final Update 2 (and Even Then, It Wasn't the End)

I have written tirelessly, endlessly, about the fact that Wisconsin's higher-ed narrative is dominated by a myth: the myth that faculty have power—the myth that faculty are so powerful that they prohibit the university from flex-o-vating nimble twenty-first-century efficiencies. I have waited patiently for Wisconsin media outlets to rely on something other than Politifact to take a stand. None of this has happened. So let me point out something to outside observers that should be breathtakingly obvious: powerful people and interests are again moving swiftly to curtail the job security of powerless people. If faculty are so powerful, the great titans of the state, why can't they simply put an end to this attack? Because the power is, and was always, held by the other parties involved: the people who cut budgets, give tax breaks, build stadiums for pungent teams, raise tuition, and collaborate with ease to extend Wisconsin's new tradition of weakening worker protections and earning power. It's that simple. So, dear media outlets, stop writing about faculty as if they are, or ever were, the source of any problem the UW has. They aren't.

Summary: those with power have invested a powerless constituency with the appearance of power (aka "divide"). They then use their real power to attack those people who, all along, were powerless to stop them (aka "conquer"). Get it? They never had the power to cause the problems they are being associated with. (*See* American workers. *Also* history.)

Another note to the media: feel free to ask President Cross some very basic questions about motive. Basic information will suffice. I have never seen someone in the center of a conflict be asked to go on the record so little about his intentions. Whether someone agrees with him or not, everyone in the UW deserves a clear, directly stated picture of what his goals are, especially if President Cross agrees that the system should weaken tenure to the point of irrelevancy. Certainly we can all agree that we should have this clear statement of vision and direction.

OK then, let's walk over to studio 2 and play "Ten Questions for President Cross." I hope that someone, somewhere in the Wisconsin media landscape, will use this as a cheat sheet— that's the real point. No one cares about the scribblings of hippy-poet bloggers. I ask these not to be antagonistic; I ask because, literally, I believe almost no one knows the answers, and clarity would be helpful.

TEN QUESTIONS FOR PRESIDENT CROSS

1. Yes or No: Are you in favor of the revised tenure guidelines that allow faculty to be fired for any of a host of reasons related to program changes?

2. Yes or No: Did you participate in, or lobby for, the creation of the revised language in the Joint Finance Committee omnibus bill? [Tenure protections were stripped in a budget bill, so there was no debate, and there were no public hearings.]

3. Yes or No: Are you supportive of requiring faculty to go through a rigorous, years-long, entirely performance-based tenure process and then allowing, upon completion of that

process, said faculty to be fired for reasons completely unrelated to their performance?

4. Yes or No: Are you comfortable with taking away existing tenure protections from faculty who earned those protections? Put another way, after asking faculty "to complete X for Y," and X has been completed by thousands of hardworking Wisconsin citizens, are you comfortable with taking away Y?

5. Yes or No: Have you, or will you, argue that all UW tenured and tenure-track faculty be grandfathered into the protections offered by the original statute, which was promised to them when you secured and benefited from their labor?

6. Yes or No: Are you willing to attempt to break an existing contract with tenured and tenure-track faculty?

7. Yes or No: You have said that if faculty can be arbitrarily fired, then there is no tenure—since tenure is earned via a grueling performance-based process, isn't the firing of any faculty member for reasons not performance based arbitrary?

8. Yes or No: Will you publicly, in full view of all UW employees, ask the Board of Regents and the Wisconsin legislature to restore tenure protections, as previously written, to state statute? (Note: even if they say no, it's probably important that our leader ask if this is indeed what he wants.)

9. Yes or No: Given your own plans for regionalization, and given incoming regent Grebe's [a Scott Walker appointee and son of the chair of Walker's gubernatorial campaigns] statement that we must cut programs,[1] and given the recent Board of Regents votes, and given that proposed tenure changes perfectly align with such plans, do you expect us to believe that there is not a plan in place to start cutting programs and thus arbitrarily firing the faculty who work in those programs?

---

1. http://www.wpr.org/uw-board-regents-candidate-suggests
-eliminating-degree-programs-some-campuses.

10. Can you, and will you, finally acknowledge that you agree with and welcome all the changes described herein? At least then we have honesty and transparency. If you do not agree and welcome these changes, can you publicly state such, thus placing the concerns and feelings of UW employees ahead of any "punishment" for daring to make a statement? Or maybe just "How do you feel about all of this?" (I guess that's more than one question.)

Bonus Questions for Media to Ask Legislators and Regents

Bonus Question 1: Yes, we know that Wisconsin is the only state with tenure written into state statute. Still, that is not a reason to change it. How, specifically, does the state benefit economically, via this budget bill, by removing these protections from statute?

Bonus Question 2: What do you hope the result of such an action will be, especially with the expanded powers related to how people can be fired? (Please answer without using the word "flexibility" or "modernization" or any of its variants.)

Bonus Question for Anyone in the Media

Bonus-Bonus Question: Have you asked anyone, and then reported on, the legality of breaking this commitment after people have given up years of their lives, and countless other job opportunities, based on that promise? Is it possible that the UW has a legal department with paid employees?

Regularly Scheduled Programming . . .

It is impossible for me to read these events any other way: the UW System is trying to pretend at tenure (warning: you will hear meaningless austerity cues like "modernize tenure" thrown about). In short, what kind of farce requires people to dedicate more than half a decade of their lives to rolling in the teeth of an exhausting, performance-based tenure metric when job security is actually in service to an entirely different, arbitrary metric? In short, why the heck would you ask anyone to go through the tenure process at all? What kind of person, what kind of moral disaster, asks people to give so much of their lives and effort simply to sweep away those years under "this program isn't aligned with the needs of this business that doesn't care about your curriculum and doesn't pay state taxes anyway"?

In one of the most bizarre developments I can think of in higher education, we are about to have one of the world's most respected university systems pretend to have tenure.

Final note: I write this from a particular point of view, that of a faculty member. Please be aware that I know the proposed changes affect academic staff and any other number of people. I care about those things just as much; I am just too ignorant of the details to write about them. If you've read any of my other work, even before the UW Update series, you'd know that I've written about adjunct labor and exploitation and about K–12 teachers. I value all those views and struggles, and I'm simply adding a specific voice to that chorus.

Eye on the Ball

GIVEN THE INTENSE FOCUS ON FACULTY, and how distant faculty are from being the source of the UW System's problems, it takes some effort to stay focused on what the real goals of our current legislature and system leadership involve. Faculty, the eternal punching bag, are to be brought to heel; austerity and automation are aggressively implemented to deliver tax cuts to the highest earners; and all of this is rhetorically normalized in our media and public discussion.

Hit the Aqueducts

I'm not one for conspiracy theories, unless they are the two that snuggle close to my heart (*Where are they hiding the dinosaurs?* and *Was Marlon Brando real?*), but a curious thing happened over the weekend. The *Milwaukee Journal Sentinel* published an interview with Speaker Robin Vos[1] that included two revealing quotes that were (insert rumble of thunder) later edited out by the deputy managing editor.

---

1. http://www.jsonline.com/news/statepolitics/robin-vos -defends-budget-provisions-on-tenure-shared-governance-b99518186z1 -307120591.html.

Although now deleted, the quotes are burned in my brain—I can paraphrase them with 100 percent accuracy—and as I said, they are revealing in a way that should give everyone, of any political affiliation, pause (if you care about education, that is). Let's file the first as an Alanis Morissette "this might be ironic depending on whether you get irony" event.

Both comments have to do with regionalization—which the legislature, President Cross, and the Board of Regents are currently collaborating on while saying they are not—but let me start with the most humorous. In short, Speaker Vos wonders why campuses must offer classes that are offered at other campuses ("access" and "demand" are apparently not applicable answers), and he tried to conjure an example that would sound obscure (think "the ancient mating habits of ur-donkeys"). The result: do we need someone who teaches "ancient Italian history" at every campus? First, I'm unclear why our republican leadership would not let the market decide such questions: if the demand is there, we should employ ten such people on every campus, no? So I have one essential question for Speaker Vos, who got his start as the owner of RoJo's Popcorn: do we really need popcorn at every movie theater? Couldn't we just have it at one or two and let the rest of the people eat Sno-Caps and black licorice? What's with all the concession duplication?

Why is this "ancient Italian history" comment important? Well, it shows a glaring lack of knowledge about real accomplishment, about the people who compose the UW and do wonderful work. What do I mean? The UW System Professor of the Year is my colleague Greg Aldrete, who teaches, and you can't make this stuff up, *ancient Italian history*. (More accurately, Greg does amazing work all around in ancient history, and he's a true treasure.) So there are two options here: either Speaker Vos doesn't know or care who the UW Professor of the Year is, or he's offended that the winner did not have a PhD in units and inventory. Greg Aldrete accepted his award at a Board of Regents meeting and made some remarks[2] as part of the ceremony. Here is a section that stood out to me:

> One of the original ideas behind the foundation of the university, when they were first created as institutions during the Middle Ages, was that exposing people to this sort of humanistic education fundamentally transformed them, and actually made them better human beings and citizens.
>
> As a historian working in an interdisciplinary humanities department, I have to confess that there is something a little bittersweet about the timing of this award. As you are all too well aware, we live in a moment when, across the nation, the value of a university education, and especially, the value of the humanities within that education, is being challenged.
>
> You are the Board of Regents, and the future of the UW System is in your hands. In whatever ways this wonderful education system ends up being transformed or changed over the coming years and decades, I hope that we never lose sight of the original core function of the university, which was to be a place in which informed, thoughtful citizens are forged, and above all, as a place where questions are asked.

Flashing forward, we can see why such remarks from a lowly humanities professor might position him for an "obscurity" jab and identification as a trouble maker. And although Madison chancellor Blank does not have the courage to say it, I will: this is a coordinated attack on the university, starting with an attempted revision of the Wisconsin Idea;[3] thoughtful citizens who ask questions are not needed in our new corporate/CEO framework. This has been stated plainly—chancellors should

2. http://news.uwgb.edu/log-news/faculty-staff/04/14/text-prof -gregory-s-aldretes-acceptance-speech-for-uw-system-teacher-of-the -year/.

3. http://www.jsonline.com/news/education/scott-walkers -uw-mission-rewrite-could-end-the-wisconsin-idea-b99439020z1 -290797681.html.

be CEOs. Search for truth? More like, shut up and get to work. This should deeply concern Wisconsinites of all political stripes. Are we not better than this? And let me be clear: this is not a "conservative" attack—true conservatives should be appalled at the current budget and decision making at all levels—it is a corporate attack that diminishes local interests, control, and expertise.

I would also ask this of our legislators: when trying to talk about what people in the UW do, what the value of that work is, is it too much to ask that you have evidence? (Tenured people don't have to show up for work? A deliberate untruth. If I don't go to work, I get fired. Also, I love my work too much not to go.) We have thousands and thousands of real human beings who are available for interview and reference, who would love to detail their expertise and contributions for you; why not reach out instead of offering groundless, abstract criticism? We're talking about real people. Instead, here's what our state has to say to a globally recognized teacher and scholar: "Hit the aqueducts pal, and don't let Cato the Elder kick you in the gluteus maximus on the way out!"

And now to the more revealing and disturbing quote. Building off the ancient Roman history comment, Speaker Vos said what I will paraphrase as follows: why not have this teacher offer the class on one campus, and then put it online for other campuses to offer, allowing us to move resources into other areas of need?

That's what he said, without ambiguity. This should frighten any conservative, libertarian, democrat, independent, and pro-Castro Wisconsinite who cares about education. Why? This illustrates, at the most fundamental level, a complete disregard for knowledge about teaching and learning. This comment is so far away from education as having learning for its goal that I simply don't know where to begin; it would be like me saying to a home builder, "Hurry up with pouring the foundation, and really, don't be concerned about water drainage at all." Put another way, this is wasteful. This is a fatal fissure in the foundation.

I have spent my entire career in the UW as a teacher of face-to-face, online, and hybrid courses—let me make the most obvious point: anyone who thinks teaching and learning are the same online as they are face-to-face is catastrophically wrong; if that person happens to reside in a position of influence, the person can inflict serious harm on students, especially those who are not yet performing at a high level. "Let's just put those courses online," specifically to "save" resources, is educational malpractice.

Let me present a *greatly* abbreviated list:

- Online education, on the level of pedagogy, requires even greater investment (think instructional design employees; course management systems; tech support employees; teachers [more employees!]; building, testing, and revising courses, etc.). You don't pursue online education so you can shift resources *away* from that teaching and learning to what you call other "high-need" areas; you pursue it because you are committed to shifting resources *to* that teaching and learning, precisely because it is a need. Put another way, a person who is incredibly influential on higher-ed policy in Wisconsin sees online learning as an "easy" endeavor that requires fewer resources. Think about that. This is the environment he, and those aligned with him, want the majority of Wisconsin students to work in: only the elite on a designated campus will have access to the face-to-face portion of the instruction. Why do I get the feeling that UW-Madison will be the home base for much of this?

- Who is one expert who knows a lot about this? Cathy Davidson. She is an education pioneer, an advocate of sound pedagogy, and someone who is anything but status quo. I've had dinner with Cathy Davidson: she is as insightful and informed in the moment as she is in prepared venues. In her recent forays into online teaching and massive open online courses (MOOCs), Davidson repeatedly came to the same conclusions: they are not less work, they are more work, and they require more labor/employees; they don't require fewer resources but more resources. Here are two of many choice quotes I could pull from Davidson's work:[4]

> The Coursera website promises "a future where everyone has access to a world-class education that has so far been available to a select few." Are my amateur lecture videos a "world-class education"? Not even close. You pay for an elite education because of the individual instruction and advising, the array of rich face-to-face experiences (with teachers and peers), conversations, labs, art exhibits, seminars, study abroad possibilities, extracurricular events, practical internships and engagement opportunities, and research experiences offered by an elite institution. Even though we strive to make our meta-MOOC as participatory as possible, a free online course can never offer all that a tuition-paying Duke student can take advantage of in the course of a semester."

And . . . [5]

> for teaching this six-week Duke-based course on The History and Future of Higher Education, I receive a stipend of $10,000, none of which will come into my own pocket. Literally. A colleague who taught one last year received a $20,000 payment and used all of it on teaching assistants, technical assistants, and equipment. Similarly, I am using 100% of my 10K stipend to support the time of some of my HASTAC colleagues who are helping me mount this

4. http://www.digitalpedagogylab.com/hybridped/10-things-learned-from-making-a-meta-mooc/.
5. https://www.hastac.org/blogs/cathy-davidson/2013/06/11/clearing-some-myths-about-moocs.

extremely complex enterprise, plus permissions for copyrighted material, some equipment, travel to film segments and conduct interviews, and many other costs, and I'm told Duke is paying for more support help this year than last (which is why I'm getting 50 percent less) but it's still not a way any prof should be moonlighting.

Yes, let's just put courses online—not to serve good pedagogy and our actual students but to save resources. Look at Davidson's words, based on real experience. Again, anyone, of any party, who cares about education in Wisconsin should be concerned about the vision hinted at in Speaker Vos's comment. Quality teaching and learning never happen on the cheap. Why are we giving up on investing in education?

- Speaker Vos's statement points to what many—conservatives and liberals alike—have feared: a plan for regionalization that creates (or further reinforces) a two-tiered public university system. We will have limited classroom access for a select group of students, and for the rest of you? Ah, we'll just throw it all online. Efficiencies! This is a moral disaster. This is class discrimination. This is dehumanizing.

- I have seen many, many examples of terrible online teaching. There are times that I have been a terrible online teacher. Almost always, the reasons for this are consistent: a belief that classrooms can be replicated online and that online teaching is somehow easier.

- Built into this, of course, are plans to exploit low-paid adjunct labor instead of paying for tenure-track and tenure-level faculty. Why else do you write a law that makes it effortless to fire such people?

- There are living human beings who do actual research on teaching and learning (Scholarship of Teaching and Learning). Some of them live in Wisconsin and work in the UW System, though you wouldn't know that, as legislators these days aren't much for consulting with teachers about

education (see K–12). So, the next time you talk with a legislator, or someone who rabidly hates the UW for some reason, ask him to name one study he's read about teaching and
learning. Ask him if it was peer reviewed. Okay, scratch that
. . . still, studies are starting to demonstrate clearly that online learning, by itself, is often not as effective as hybrid and
face-to-face environments, especially for students who need
the most help.[6] So, do we have no moral imperative? Do we
only want to serve the elite? All forces indicate that no, we
have no moral imperative. We're simply giving up on education in the face of austerity, which strangles the imagination
and offers no dreams or vision beyond "cut, less, flexibility,
efficiency, shutter this." How bleak. Aren't we embarrassed
to aim so low and to court what is so easy?

Speaking of easy, there is a lot of talk about efficiency and
wasting resources. Is it not the greatest waste of all to ignore
your in-house experts? The UW System, filled with expertise
and knowledge, is ignored as a resource by legislators and UW
Central administration alike. Why? Well, input is not needed
when the completely inflexible, inefficient vision is already in
place. We've completely turned away from each other. Isn't
that the point of the recent "reforms" to tenure and shared
governance—to minimize input, and democracy, in the guise of
"flexibility"? Vos himself aptly uses the word "dictate" in this
Milwaukee Journal Sentinel piece: "I have supported shared
governance in an advisory role. But it has evolved to instead of
offering advice, having the ability to decide and dictate." What
is there to say? If the role of other constituencies is merely advisory, then governance is not shared. And his solution to seeing
constituencies "dictate"? Install a different dictator. Democracy

6. http://www.careerladdersproject.org/docs/Online%20
Learning.pdf.

is great for campaigning but not so much in actual practice, where it's just too hard and inconvenient and inefficient.

We are not going to succeed unless we first recognize the responsibility that rests on all our shoulders and then move that responsibility ahead of the chips that sit in its way.

The Banality of Weasels

This has been, to say the least, a disheartening year. Again, public servants—with teachers often at the forefront—have been demonized in the latest round of "grownups playing public relations." When budget decisions are made in June (maybe), most teachers won't even be under contract, opting instead to retreat to their accessorized yachts and mansions on various tropical, taxpayer-funded islands. Personally, I and various rappers will retire to my brand-new yacht, which I've christened *Union Thug without Collective Bargaining Rights of Any Kind*. I live large.

But let me get to the point. For those who catch the reference in my title, I greatly admire Hannah Arendt. She demystified for me the figure of the evil genius and the master plan. She focused on the "unthinking," the middle manager who, beyond a specific competency, might as well have been Mr. Magoo. And thus Wisconsin, where most people don't know what they are doing—and here lies another desperate and fanciful call for voters to help rectify this.

So, where are we in the great unthinking budget games?

Exhibit A: Let's start outside of the UW for a moment, where a state legislator has pretty much said we should cut the science

bureau of the state's Department of Natural Resources.[7] Why? Climate change, of course! Like many other parts of the country, opposition to the reality of climate change, or that humans have direct effects on the environment, passes as "thinking" or a "point of view." To quote the senator in question, "I'm critical of science services. I don't think they've used good science. And I've got to tell you, they've done big-time harm here to my district here in northern Wisconsin."

Good science! Let me get this straight: if you think scientists are bad at their jobs, you don't get better scientists, you simply get rid of scientists in total. I sympathize. For example, when we had a plumbing problem at home, where a pipe broke and spewed waste all over the basement, we weren't sure if that waste had come from humans or not. After all, it was coming out of a pipe and not someone's body. Given that, I fired all plumbers in my mind. We now just live in our own filth and connect to a simpler time.

Exhibit B: The *Wisconsin State Journal* just ran an article on the "uncertain" future of tenure and shared governance in the UW System.[8] If there's any issue that has been talked about with more deep ignorance and unthinking, it's the concept of tenure. OK, maybe health care, death camps, and the impending U.S. takeover of Texas, but tenure is up there. Honestly, this stultifying incompetence amounts to this recurring discussion, in full. Tell me if you've heard it before: "Jobs for life! Fire people! Teach more, you lazy sloth!"

7. http://lacrossetribune.com/news/state-and-regional/sen-tom-tiffany-says-he-asked-governor-for-dnr-job/article_91e474d3-aea0-58fc-b1e9-d7cc048e9d2a.html.

8. http://host.madison.com/wsj/news/local/govt-and-politics/tenure-shared-governance-at-uw-face-uncertain-future-as-legislature/article_f7aaed63-dfde-5836.

Is it possible, just once, for a reporter, or a UW official, or a legislator, to mention, say, accreditation and the role tenure plays in having accredited programs, and why that would be a requirement? That's just a suggestion that requires someone out there to be among the thinking, to know something. We'll just let the deciders step in and have a word:

> [Assembly Speaker] Vos recently doubled down on his criticism, saying he was withdrawing support for Walker's proposed UW public authority in part because the Board of Regents had passed resolutions to protect tenure and shared governance.
>
> "Why are we giving you the autonomy to do nothing with it if you're going to protect the status quo?" he said in an interview with WisconsinEye.

Let's me get this straight: "We have to cut your budget because of a monetary shortfall—there's nothing we can do about that! However, we won't help you alleviate the monetary situation because you hold the 'status quo' on these entirely nonproblematic, nonmonetary things." Got it.

Now, let us pause and ask what the thinking people do: let's say tenure and shared governance were problems, as some legislators have indicated. Would one offer, maybe, an example? If not, maybe just offer up a question that would require an example? Indeed:

> By contrast, Assembly Speaker Robin Vos, R-Rochester, has harshly criticized the joint decision-making process. Vos took aim at shared governance during a forum in 2013, saying the balance of power in decision-making needed to be tilted more toward chancellors, allowing them to act as campus CEOs.
>
> "Does the role of allowing faculty to make a huge number of decisions help the system or hurt the system?" he asked.

So, a question has been asked here. With the position presented here so firmly in the negative, we are ready for examples to follow. None are given. What is offered as thinking? "More like

CEO's . . . the boss . . . power." I wonder if people do actual research on such things? Who would those people be, and where might we find them? Hmmm . . .

Summary: Although, as admitted by President Ray Cross, all shared governance is advisory, we should empower chancellor CEOs to make decisions about . . . advice? Wisconsin has a ton of solutions looking for problems.

Exhibit C: State leaders, who are all about the middle class and helping people get access to affordable education, rejected a student loan refinancing proposal.[9] Here is the dynamic wisdom of how to solve this problem:

> Nygren and Sen. Sheila Harsdorf, R-River Falls, both said colleges ought to focus on making sure students graduate on time, and that students should consider which degrees will help them pay off their debt.
> The degree a student chooses likely has more impact on debt and the ability to pay it off than any other factor, Nygren said.

That makes complete sense! Thinking! As we all know, there are no important professions that require a college degree while not landing you in the country-club boardroom. You know, mildly important things like social work, journalism, and agriculture. But there is a budding major in a new field called "automatic profit from everything you do"! Also, get your degree faster while we construct budgets that cut positions and course offerings.

9. http://host.madison.com/ct/news/local/govt-and-politics /wisconsin-budget-committee-rejects-student-loan-refinancing -proposal/article_af41a0c6-ec22-51ca-b61b-c6dbcb3c8813.html.

Summary: Education is valuable only if you are wealthy with plans to continue being wealthy.

Exhibit D: Every piece of empty rhetoric you've heard from upper administration. Can anyone possibly zombify her way through another "listening session"? I recently heard the phrase "the humanities are going to have to get on board!" With what? Teaching humanities curriculum? Making the university a profit with our full classes and waiting lists?

Still, I'll ask, how is the "behind closed doors" strategy working out down at Central for President Ray Cross? Now, there is a "resignation" plot that the press keeps referring to, and given the recent news about revenue, about restoring K–12 funding, lessening the cut to public broadcasting, all while not bringing in any new revenue, things look bleak. To be honest, I have little to no hope of good outcomes for education in a landscape of grudges and prideful simplicity. And when those bad outcomes arrive, we'll have had no look at the mechanisms. How effective were the backroom conversations that people like me are too immature and unimportant to be privy to? I'd say, going forward, that I'm about as fond of this rhetorical (non)strategy as I am of gas-station hot dogs. It is gross and uninspiring.

I feel we are at the point where real ideas are offensive. When was the last time, in relation to the UW budget, that you heard meaningful discussion? Instead, just major in wealth, something tenure, you're not ready for autonomy or lobotomy, science is for losers, Rebecca Blank is mean, and "don't worry, the big cheeses got this covered." Here's the reality about "tough decisions": doing what you always planned to do is easy; going against the ideological crowd, changing your mind to do good—that's tough.

I'll make one point about public servants and the UW: the situation we are in, right now, as a system, is the result of a lot of people doing their jobs poorly and predictably. For as much flack as UW faculty and staff (and students) receive, here's a news flash—they're the only ones who did their jobs this year and excelled. We are now at the end of the academic year. Faculty and staff did their jobs. It's time for some other folks to do theirs.

Horseshit Preemption Edition

As expected, there will be no new revenue to help alleviate violent cuts to various Wisconsin public services and institutions.[10] Let's preempt our planned horseshit-water rafting excursion—a deliverance, if you will, from the oncoming tide of lies about "tough choices" that supposedly appear via magic rather than their own deliberate set of calculations.

We can begin with the article footnoted earlier, especially this supper club–sized serving: "Republican leaders have stood firmly against raising taxes, leaving them few sustainable options except to make cuts."[11] Journalism! Let's rephrase: *because of a nonbinding choice entirely in their control, they have no control.* Got it.

And let the "tough choices" gnashing of teeth begin.

Announcement: there are no tough choices now. The choices were already made, and the results perfectly match the desired outcomes. Lower tax revenue = smaller government; therefore, freedom! At the very least, media outlets, let's not pretend that revenue shortfalls are a sudden change in unpredictable weath-

10. http://www.jsonline.com/news/statepolitics/no-hike-in -revenue-estimates-forces-tough-budget-decisions-b99495357z1 -302763911.html.
11. Ibid.

er. They are the result of deliberate policy and deliberate choices. What we have now are not "tough choices." What we have are tough results.

A current *Milwaukee Journal Sentinel* headline reads, "No Hike in Revenue Estimates Forces Tough Budget Decisions." Let me rewrite the headline to not make excuses for people and circumstances that have clear, identifiable causes: "State Revenue, Declining because of Tax Cuts, Allows Leaders to Move Forward with Desired Cuts to State Services and Institutions." There is no "forcing" involved.

And here's a reminder: when the "choice" you must make is your desired outcome, it is not tough. Got it? When buildings fall, let's not make martyrs of the architects.

Here's another reminder: this is all about money. It has always been about money and the ideological reorganization of who has access to it. So tenure, shared governance, cash reserves something or other, all relate to this budget . . . how?

We pause for an interview with Chuck Rybak! An important man who was generous enough to put down his coffee and speak with us!

CHUCK: How will any alteration of policies related to tenure and shared governance affect the current budget situation?

CHUCK: They won't. There is no monetary connection whatsoever. Strike that. Shared governance does save money,[12] so it's probably more important now than ever. Furthermore, tenure is free, and likely the only thing preventing highly skilled faculty from leaving the UW for even moderately higher pay.

CHUCK: Then why do people spend so much time talking about these things?

12. http://www.jsonline.com/news/opinion/university-of -wisconsin-system-needs-accountability-for-everyone-b99463142z1 -296507081.html.

CHUCK: Don't ask me [*pregnant pause*], but I do have ideas about why people would give the appearance of completely unconnected issues being connected.

CHUCK: What could happen, in terms of choices, that might help the citizens of Wisconsin?

CHUCK: Hmmm. Accepting federal money for health care. Raising tax revenue by tapping those most able to pay it and those who most benefit from a system of public education. Remember, the majority of Wisconsin corporations pay no state taxes at all. Even a little would help.

CHUCK: You mean, nothing related to tenure, shared governance, or charter schools?

CHUCK: Excuse me?

CHUCK: Thanks so much for stopping by.

CHUCK: No problem. Have a nice day.

Here is your guide for dealing with media and opinion from here until the final budget is passed:

1. *There are no tough choices.* The choices that have produced this situation were already made by the very same people in question.

2. *There are no tough choices.* The preceding is very important for accountability (buzzword, I know). Let's make this an election issue now: deliberate policy has deliberately weakened education in Wisconsin. Easy choices for them; hard results for everyone else.

3. *There are no tough choices.* Push against any rhetorical horseshit that positions the upcoming cuts as a situation that "just appeared," hanging in the sky as if a distant sun we cannot reach. Our current leadership—in the Capitol and UW Central—deliberately brought us here. That's the starting point of all discussion: "specific choices by these specific people have us in this specific situation."

If the results are not good for Wisconsin and its citizens, the decision makers should be held immediately accountable. You know, just like they expect of teachers.

The beatings will continue until morale improves.

No Confidence

WITH NO OTHER OPTIONS AVAILABLE, and no power at their disposal, the faculty and staff utilized the only option remaining them, even if that option's force was purely symbolic: the no-confidence vote. Faculty, and some staff, at various campuses throughout the system passed no-confidence resolutions in both system president Ray Cross and the UW Board of Regents, using those votes to encourage the president and the regents to recommit themselves to the Wisconsin Idea and the spirit of public education. People are still debating the effects of those votes, yet one thing remains undeniable: they shifted the discussion.

The Gong Show

What if I told you that someone with responsibility literally brought a red button to a meeting? What if I told you that this person, while his subordinates were making test-run presentations, would push the button, and the words "no whining!" would be ejaculated as a sound effect? Again: this is not a metaphor. This is real.

So I'll ask: who is this person? What do you imagine the setting to be? Are we talking about adults? Younger people? A gimmicky corporate setting? Friday night neon bowling?

No. That would be the president of the UW System, and the subordinates would be our campus chancellors, who were asked to describe the campus effects of another *quarter-billion-dollar cut to state support*. They were instructed not to whine (as faculty have been told not to be emotional), and upon further review, *the presentations themselves were cancelled.*[1] I know what you're thinking: *this can't be true, no way; this is the president of a university system!* I know; that's what I thought as well. Here is the incident in question detailed by Nico Savidge:

"[The presentations] should be factual, not whiny," Cross wrote in his message.

> Cross insisted on this point—he said in the interview *he brought a red button to the meeting to be used if he felt a chancellor was complaining too much in a presentation. When he pressed the button, a sound effect shouted, "No whining!"* (emphasis mine, because wow)

What, were hand buzzers and bottles of seltzer spray unavailable? You couldn't find someone on a unicycle to ride up and poke them in the eyes? Look, I miss Benny Hill too, but I have access to YouTube.

Still, this can't be true. So I asked Nico on Twitter to confirm:

> @ChuckRybak that's what Cross described, yes. Did the sound effect over the phone too[2]

Can you imagine, just for a moment, being a chancellor of a university—a position with an enormous amount of responsibility to an incredibly wide range of stakeholders—and have someone interrupt you with a "no whining!" sound effect while you are

---

1. http://host.madison.com/news/local/education/university /article_b6ea2863-3bae-5895-8be2-e102951d8bf5.html.
2. Nico Savidge (@NSavidge), April 7, 2016, https://twitter.com /NSavidge/status/718062029269958656.

trying to describe how many staff members you've had to lay off and what programs you'll be cutting, with no end in sight? Would you have an existential moment of crisis where your inner voice conceded, "Oh my god, I'm an adult"? Well, I guess the "flexibility" everyone wants for chancellors doesn't apply to their speaking without permission and an approved message.

For the record, I really respect my chancellor and want him to be able to speak freely and honestly about his responsibilities. He is far too classy ever to complain about such a stunt, but I have no class, and thus at the first press of the button, I would have immediately gone over the table.

Unfortunately, none of this is a joke.

Right now, the Board of Regents is meeting on my campus, pleasantly hosted by a great number of people they just stripped earned job protections away from. They will have the best parking spots and eat for free. A large portion of the Cloud Commons, where just two nights ago students had to wait in line past 9:00 P.M. to cast their votes, will be blocked off and reserved for this meeting—the regents will wait for nothing.

What is today's meeting all about? The continuance of the big lie(s). Right now, a few of those include the following:

1. The most important strategy for our future budgets is tone policing. Nico Savidge reported that the presentations were cancelled "after consulting with some Regents and considering, among other factors, the system's next two-year budget." False. Reducing money for all things public is a feature, not a bug, and *more cuts are coming no matter what we say or do.* Don't believe me? I suggest you begin making regular stops over at *Jake's place,*[3] where he dives into the deep,

3. http://jakehasablog.blogspot.com/.

deep numbers, *like this coming disaster*:[4] "If the tax-season months of March and April don't have a bounce-back and stay below trend, it will be likely that the 2016–17 fiscal year budget will have to be repaired . . . even with $726 million in unspecified lapses built into that budget."

2. We have "comparable" and "often better" tenure policies than our peers. This lie has been repeated so often that it's moving past "big." We don't have tenure anymore. We wear a button that says "tenure" until that button is taken away, for any reason you can imagine. *That's been the point all along.* That's also why, whether we whine or not, whether we are emotional or not, more cuts are coming. The reason you strip away people's job security, other than welcoming them to the twenty-first century, is to begin removing those people. That removal will be dressed up in the language of "necessity" and "tough choices," that is, budget cuts. But I get it: the illusion of prestige will be necessary for some to come to work.

But somehow this is all a joke or a gag, worthy of a buzzer; was someone tasked with securing a "no whining" button? I can't help but think what this models for our students and communities and whether anyone cares anymore. We did, after all, just elect a supreme court justice in Wisconsin whose main workplace qualification is intolerance. The Rebecca Bradley apologists sang a constant chorus that is relevant to this blog post: *those were just college rantings, who wants to be held responsible for their silly college-age thoughts? We grow out of that.*

The implication: what college students say should not be taken seriously. But not only is it our job and responsibility to take them seriously, it is our mission.

What students think and feel matters today, and it will mat-

4. http://jakehasablog.blogspot.com/2016/03/february-revneues-collapse-wisconsin.html.

ter tomorrow. When students interrupted the previous Board of Regents meeting with a chant of protest, the regent who was speaking at the time *rolled his eyes*. I was watching the live feed. He rolled his eyes at students who dared to speak out of turn. When the meeting resumed, the regents gave themselves yet another round of applause for their hard work, which amounts to a speck of dust when compared with the tenure dossiers of the faculty they swiftly moved to devalue.

So what are we being taught by our central leadership?

Speaking honestly about the effects of another round of brutal cuts is whining. Fighting to preserve job protections, which are an earned property right, is being emotional. (What, after all, is a life's work worth anyway?) And if you're a student, or worse, a graduate who has significant debt, learn to be responsible! And these complaints about race and gender issues . . . silly young coddled college kids.

What is the value of a coordinated message that pretends that everything is OK? At what point is it just blatantly dishonest, and who, outside of the UW, will point that out?

I'm not asking for miracles, because I'm a realist and I know what is coming. Still, I don't think it's too much to ask for our system president to take us seriously, to not belittle the beleaguered, to not scold the scapegoated, and to consider, just once, standing with UW employees, even if it means stepping out from behind the great "thank you" emblazoned on our flimsy, rhetorical shield.

The No-Confidence Man

So here's where we are—the faculty at UW-Madison are considering a "no-confidence" vote in system president Ray Cross and the Board of Regents. For the record, I am not on the faculty at Madison and would not dare to offer whether this is the right course of action; that's for them to decide. But here's what I can say—the mere specter of such a vote has unleashed complete buffoonery and a stampede of frothing jamokies. Holy smokes. There are two popular themes at this blog, but let me iterate them just for the heck of it: (1) faculty are always to blame and (2) you won't believe what happened since the last thing that happened.

Since the moment Pandora's word escaped from the box of a possible no-confidence vote, we have had the Madison chancellor's blogged response,[5] a legislator's first response,[6] and another legislator's not-so-veiled-threat release,[7] followed by two legislators issuing a joint falsehood[8]—all with the same themes: *freedom, taxpayers, I love my family, Kohl's cash, you'll regret this, in the real world.*

Also of note: no-confidence resolutions are a perfectly legitimate part of governance, BUT COMPLETELY NONBINDING, AND THEY LITERALLY HAVE ZERO IMPACT ON POLICY! But as we like to say at my home, whatevs.

In other words, WHEREAS I might have some shit to say, and WHEREAS I'm saying that shit right now, THEREFORE BE IT RESOLVED that you don't have to listen to me or do anything as a result.

It's a fancy way of offering an opinion that has pretty much already been made clear by the hordes of unwashed, downtrodden folks in the halls of learning.

But what the heck is going on that's got everyone's beans on the grill?

5. https://chancellor.wisc.edu/blog/looking-ahead-to-may -faculty-senate/.
6. http://legis.wisconsin.gov/assembly/05/steineke/news /rep-steineke-statement-on-uw-madison-faculty-s-no-confidence -resolution/.
7. https://www.wispolitics.com/index.iml?Article=369727.
8. http://www.thewheelerreport.com/wheeler_docs/files /0427nygrendarling.pdf.

Wisconsin Madness Summary! (Look for the Trend)

CALL: Faculty speak out against move to a public authority.
RESPONSE: We're not listening.

CALL: Faculty speak out against budget cuts.
RESPONSE: Who cares, we're not listening.

CALL: Faculty protest attack on tenure/earned property right.
RESPONSE: Not listening.

CALL: Faculty speak against limitations in shared governance.
RESPONSE: I can't hear you.

CALL: Faculty ask for effects of cuts to be publicly presented.
RESPONSE: Not listening. Also, "no whining!"

CALL: Faculty propose amendments to tenure/layoff statutes.
RESPONSE: Did you say something?

CALL: Faculty ask Ray Cross for an iota of public support.
RESPONSE: Can't hear you.

CALL: Faculty at Madison propose a no-confidence vote in people who have completely ignored everything faculty have had to say about anything . . .

RESPONSE: Don't, because people are listening! Or . . . OH MY PETUNIAS, HOW DARE YOU PROPOSE A NONBINDING DOCUMENT AFTER WE'VE BLUDGEONED YOU WITH ACTUAL LEGISLATION AND IGNORED YOU COMPLETELY! GET OUT THE FAINTING COUCHES! WATCH YOUR TONE, YOU UPPITY BOOKNUT, OR NO DONUTS OR BUDGET FOR YOU! EVER!

Wait . . . what? Does this strike anyone else as profoundly weird? (Remember: this post is about "confidence.")

So let me get this straight: after completely ignoring faculty concerns at nearly every turn, after abandoning faculty to incessant attacks from all comers, after remaining silent on fake "studies surveys" on tenure, after painting your faculty as "emotional" for reacting to the loss of earned job protections, after taking over every branch of government possible and stacking the Board of Regents with corporate hatchets . . . suddenly UW Central and the legislature are upset about a no-confidence motion that they could completely ignore as they have done everything else? What? Why?

The thing is, the deeper you dig, the more confusing things get, as in people don't know what they're talking about. Do you want examples?

OK, the first response is Chancellor Rebecca Blank. She doesn't issue press releases; she takes her word directly to the streets via her blog. Among her claims: "Such a vote would put the UW-Madison faculty in opposition to our governing board, with which we work closely and must have a positive relationship." Basically, doing this will lead to a political backlash that will result in more budget cuts. (This is the "faculty are always to blame" trump card, which is synonymous with "shut up.")

But none of this makes sense—there is no "relationship" with the Board of Regents because there is no dialogue, no reciprocity, and really no interest beyond achieving the predetermined ends of the austerity agenda. What "relationship" do you have with officials who offer "welcome to the twenty-first century" as a justification for demeaning people's entire professional record and accomplishment?

Furthermore, and I'll say it again, this has *nothing* to do with faculty. Do you know what budgets are slightly connected to? (Ding!) Revenue. You know what Wisconsin is not interested in? (Ding!) Collecting revenue. Therefore, budget cuts. We could literally change the name of the UW System to the "Ayn Rand Academy of William Buckley's Wet Dreams on AM Radio" and we'd still see a budget cut. Lastly, are we dealing with adults anymore? Does the fate of our state's treasured university system—an essential economic, educational, and public resource—hinge on someone's tone on any given Tuesday? Really? None of this makes sense.

The second to respond was Assemblyman Jim Steineke. He reacted on Twitter, then issued his press release, which itself is hard to interpret. I'd expect someone to respond, but why him? Among his claims: that irregular UW-Madison faculty think they are better than regular folks and that the motion displays "a complete disconnect between UW-Madison faculty who seem to expect their job to come with a forever guarantee and the average Wisconsin family struggling just to make ends meet." OK, I'm confused. Why is a GOP legislator pointing out that the *average* Wisconsin family is struggling financially when we've lived under ruling-party economic policy, for a long time running, that was supposed to fix all that? A knee-jerk response might be "it's Obama's fault." But the Wisconsin economy has been underperforming when compared to national averages. Also of note: this press release doesn't seem to criticize UW-Madison as much as it works to make the following claim—the more people we have just making ends meet, the better; if you are above that state of existence, we need to bring you back down to struggling. I honestly have no idea what any of this has to do with, well, anything. None of this makes sense.

Then there's Senator Steve Nass, who has already gotten everything he wants and then some, expressing outrage (as he did when Ray Cross agreed to meet with students of color): "The radical faculty at UW-Madison are rejecting the values and expectations of the people of Wisconsin. They are backhanding the middle-class families who are pleading for controls on tuition and an end to wasteful spending in the UW System. Passage of the resolution will prove that even more institutional reforms are urgently needed and must be included in the next state budget to protect tuition-paying students." What? This is the person who has voted for massive cuts to the system, repeatedly. Tuition control? Legislators *do nothing but brag about their long-standing tuition freeze.* The best way to lower tuition? Fund tuition decreases. Backhanding the middle class? This person votes against labor protections and helped pass "right to work earn less" legislation. Do I really need to say that faculty have nothing to do with tuition policy or budgets? Do I need to point out that faculty don't have power over their own workplace, let alone the ability to backhand the entire middle class with invisible powers? Furthermore, professors pay taxes and are largely middle- to lower-middle class earners. None of this makes any sense.

OK, now Darling and Nygren, who add this whopping un-truth: "Aside from these two changes, the Regents' tenure pol-icy is virtually identical to what Wisconsin's tenure policy had been prior to Act 55." Guys. Come on. Do I really have to say this: our state legislature does not make "changes" to law that accomplish nothing. Don't you remember, the whole point is "Big and Bold." So what we're to believe here is that the com-pletely Republican-controlled state government passed laws, RELATED TO THE DREADED PROFESSORS, that did . . . nothing? Ha!

None of this makes any sense. Of all things, and of all times, why now? Why the heavy rhetorical artillery in relation to a small thing, this potential vote of no confidence, that is com-pletely nonbinding? Why these specific people, issuing releases and official documents (or blogs)? Does anyone have an idea what generated this full-court press, and is Central reaching out to these folks to do so? (A respected dirty hippy colleague of mine has convinced me that this is likely.)

But why? Our local press applies almost no heat at all to President Cross. These legislative statements praise him after, well, decimating the budget and eroding labor protections. What's the problem?

One answer, of course, is the usual: scapegoat faculty just as the public are starting to wake up to the effects of the budget cuts. It's too bad people actually have to lose something to snap out of it, but people are starting to notice, and with the Trump candidacy looming, maybe folks are getting a bit nervous about their seats and need a quick reset to divide-and-conquer mode—that feels like what's going on, as seen in the usual "make ends meet working class elite arrogant liberty" rhetoric at work. But maybe there's something else. If there is, I hope someone writes about it.

In terms of the potential vote itself, it doesn't really matter much to me. Why? The phrase "no confidence" just feels redundant at this point.

TL; DR

For the past few years I've used this space to be a reporter of sorts. I have reported on events, while also indulging my Carveresque appetite for exploring how we talk about things. The results have been mixed in that each revelation immediately shoulders the great ecclesiastical weight of "there is nothing new under the sun": only people with money matter; power sides with power; top-down authority nurtures incompetence; the platitudes of leadership apply to everyone but leadership; faculty are always the bottom rung; [insert your own maxim that is both contemporary and timeless]. What else is there to say? A lot, I hope. Let me strip this post of humor and video and memes and just talk about what's missing in Wisconsin: truth, honesty.

Let me offer this openly—there are a lot of people lying about the current state of the UW System. Many have had their lying documented in print, the kind of documentation where you can put two quotes from the same speaker side by side and see that they are opposites. No one seems to care about lying all that much anymore—our culture more than tolerates it—thus reinforcing the two irrefutable truths this blog relies on: faculty are always to blame and you won't believe what's happened since the last thing that happened. But if "basic to every purpose of the system is the search for truth," then I suggest we start telling the truth as a means for discovering it.

In a little detour, yesterday I was reading the text of a Rebecca Solnit speech to journalism students that focused on how to find the real stories hiding within dominant, mainstream, or moneyed-interest narratives. The piece is called "To Break the Story You Must Break the Status Quo,"[9] and I was particularly struck by this passage as it might apply to the UW System:

> I think of the mainstream media as having not so much a right-wing or leftwing bias but a status-quo bias, a tendency to believe people in authority, to trust institutions and corporations and the rich and powerful . . . to let people who have been proven to tell lies tell more lies that get reported without questioning, to move forward on cultural assumptions that are readily disproved, and to devalue nearly all outsiders, whether they're discredited or mocked or just ignored.

I challenge anyone to deny that this accurately describes the rhetorical reality of the UW narrative right now. What is the most glaring proof of all? The tooth-and-nail resistance to the narrative shift caused by the no-confidence votes[10] at campuses across the system. Faculty and staff in the UW, having been

9. http://lithub.com/to-break-the-story-you-must-break-the-status-quo/.

10. http://host.madison.com/news/local/education/university/on-campus-uw-colleges-faculty-approve-no-confidence-vote/article_61fee8aa-04dd-56d8-a564-0587b8ba2162.html.

thoroughly abandoned by central leadership, are entirely on their own. Although the vast majority of those in power in Wisconsin have ignored faculty at every step of the process, something about these votes has struck a nerve, and a highly coordinated response against these completely nonbinding resolutions is the result: the system president, regents, various chancellors, newspaper editors, legislators, "think" tanks, punditry, boards of trustees, and even some students make up a mere portion of the "be quiet" chorus, and the term *status quo* is often invoked, as if speaking against traditional top-down authority and against investing wealth with even more power somehow represents a desire to preserve rather than change.

Another characteristic of the intense backlash against faculty/staff for their recent votes is the usual parade of language that includes words/phrases like *common sense, modest, in line with our peers.* So here's my question: if this is all so "common sense" and "modest," then why do you have to lie so much about process and intentions? Why are people who drone on about "accountability" for others allowed to act without any accountability to the institutions they are supposed to represent? The obvious answer is that none of this is modest or relies on common sense, but let's document some things first. (I'm aware that people using the word "lie" or "lying" is seen as uncivil and oh so beyond the pale. But I'm more literal about it: you're either lying, or you're not.)

So, yesterday the Governor's Office finally released documents related to their attempt to change the language of the Wisconsin Idea. At the time, the governor attributed this all to a mistake and a "drafting error," and the current documents confirm that this was a lie. Even when the claim was first made, Politifact Wisconsin labeled it "Pants on Fire." Let us not forget that the two words that precede "pants on fire"[11] in the traditional children's expression are "liar, liar." Instead, the documents reveal that the process was being "driven by the Governor's office" and that "the Gov requested a simplified and clearer mission and purpose statements."[12] If all of this is so minor, why lie about it?

Also aligning against faculty is system president Ray Cross. And though people are outraged that faculty might voice displeasure in the system president, none of the stories about the no-confidence votes asks if anyone, anywhere, should have confidence in someone who has lied to them and had that lie documented. What am I talking about? As I wrote before, President Cross's go-to rhetorical device was that the tenure statutes had "simply moved"[13] and that there were no substantive changes. But what did yet another Freedom of Information Act request reveal in an e-mail? That they hadn't "simply moved." In fact, he wrote, "This program discontinuance debate has exposed *the real value of removing tenure-related policies* from statutory language." The public statement was blatantly dishonest, while the more private e-mail illustrates what everyone knew to be the truth. So again, if what you're doing is so right and common sense based, why lie about it? In what ways are you accountable and "transparent" in this?

The Board of Regents is clearly aligned against faculty (that was the sole purpose for many of their appointments), and they have the power to enact changes without apology. In fact, they

11. http://www.politifact.com/wisconsin/statements/2015/feb/06/scott-walker/despite-deliberate-actions-scott-walker-calls-chan/.

12. http://cdn.wrn.com/wp-content/uploads/2016/05/052716WisconsinIdeaemails.pdf, 35.

13. http://archive.jsonline.com/news/education/regents-panel-advances-tenure-police-to-mixed-reviews-b99664974z1-367869591.html.

can state what they want to do, why, and then do it. Yet they still lie about it. For example, the Board of Regents went through the usual dishonest circus that surrounds predetermined outcomes: *we have many people participating, we're listening,* and so on. They made a big show of being "open to suggestions"[14] on wording changes to policy. This of course was another lie, as documented by the *Capital Times*,[15] with the key contradiction being "staying on message and *tamping down opposition on the tenure issue were priorities for top UW system officials.* . . . Regent Tim Higgins messaged Behling and regent president Regina Millner that day about *putting off the entreaties* of the UW-Whitewater leader of a system-wide effort to amend tenure policy proposals before the vote. 'I believe that it's important that all Regents *support the task force recommendations as presented,'* Higgins wrote." Again, if this is all so common sense and modest, why lie about it all? Why is it more important to hold faculty accountable for telling the truth?

And the lies go on and on: deliberate misrepresentations of faculty-to-student ratios,[16] deliberate misrepresentations of the decline in state support[17] for higher education, lies about "jobs for life," out toward infinity. It never stops. Still, even though faculty/staff have consistently told the truth throughout this entire process, almost no one sides with us, ever. Why? I'm tempted to refer to the preceding Solnit quote and talk about our deep fetishizing of power and "the boss," but I don't want to sound academic (that's something one has to apologize for).

14. Ibid.

15. http://host.madison.com/ct/news/local/education/university /quiet-influence-behind-the-scenes-regent-john-behling-led-the/article _193fc224-5ce8-5208-8037-4bb5970eff6e.html.

16. http://www.politifact.com/wisconsin/statements/2016/may/13 /scott-walker/scott-walker-way-saying-university-wisconsin-milwa/.

17. http://jakehasablog.blogspot.com/.

But let me suggest to anyone out there, regardless of political stripes, at least to ask herself why people who claim recent changes are "no big deal" continually have to lie about them, all while clambering for accountability. If I'm going to go to the store to buy carrots and milk, I say I'm going to the store to buy carrots and milk. It's no big deal. It's common sense (I need those things), and it's modest ($4.00). I don't scapegoat one of my kids for needing to go ("She always spills all the milk!").

Of course, the lying does serve a purpose—it distracts from other stories that might shift the narrative to unpleasant places and upset the status quo. For example:

- Not one media story I can find, not one, addresses that UW faculty who already have tenure have been stripped of an earned property right. Put another way, if there's anything I can think of that is antithetical to true conservative governance, it's taking away people's earned property/compensation. You might not like professors, but I think something people dislike even more is government taking away property/compensation that people have *already earned*. That is exactly what is happening in Wisconsin now. This is a story. It has yet to be told. It will take a shift in narrative and a brave media for that to happen, thus the hard push to paint middle-class, hardworking faculty as "out of touch."

- Not one story I can find, anywhere, addresses dishonesty as a commonsense reason for a no-confidence resolution. The dishonesty has been documented. So I'll ask anyone out there, regardless of his job: would you have confidence in a boss or authority who lied to you? This is really a simple yes-or-no question.

- Instead of fetishizing how many people get fired, or even wanting people fired, will a media outlet shift discussion toward the lengthy, beyond thorough hiring process the system must go through for *each* faculty hire? There's a reason a lot of people don't get fired—the hiring process is one of the most thorough and time consuming in the world, and we should be praised for that (even if it can be cumbersome). That's a story waiting to be told.

- Traditional media outlets are unwilling to take on Governor Walker's deliberately dishonest claim that the UW System's budget is bigger than ever, even when he doesn't account for inflation. Instead, we have to rely on resourceful, thorough bloggers like Jake[18] (the best blog going) and actual data provided by the Center on Budget and Policy Priorities,[19] which verified, "In fact, if you exclude the shifted funding responsibility for the technical college system—which appears as additional state support—state funding for Wisconsin's public two- and four-year institutions has fallen *by roughly 25 percent per student since 2008.* This includes large-scale higher education cuts from Wisconsin lawmakers in 2015, including a $250 million cut[20] to the University of Wisconsin System that caused harmful ripple effects[21] on many of the system's campuses." This is a story that needs to be told. It's waiting. It's not a "point of view." It's a story that won't permit Governor Walker to take credit for federal aid (which he usually abhors) and student-paid tuition as part of a "budget."

- When will we move past the lie that the majority of UW professors are overpaid (they are not[22]) and that by unequivocally siding with President Cross and the regents, you are siding against spoiled, overprotected faculty. This is a lie. In

18. http://jakehasablog.blogspot.com/2016/05/how-higher-ed -increase-led-to-higher-ed.html.

19. http://www.cbpp.org/blog/wisconsin-higher-ed-funding-shift -inflated-state-support.

20. https://www.washingtonpost.com/news/answer-sheet/wp /2015/07/13/gov-scott-walker-savages-wisconsin-public-education-in -new-budget/.

21. http://www.wisconsinbudgetproject.org/wp-content/uploads /2015/05/2015-UW-Cuts1.pdf.

22. http://chuckrybak.com/wp-content/uploads/2016/05/Pay-Gap .png.

fact, the pattern is quite the opposite: in standing against UW faculty/staff, people *always* side with people who make more money and have more job security. I will use myself as an example: my starting salary in the UW System, with a PhD, was $40,000. At nearly *15 years* in, I am just now hitting $50,000 with a family of four. To go over 50K, I must take overload assignments, secure stipends for research-related work, and so on. Several my graduating students earn starting salaries that exceed my current pay (which I'm very happy for). News flash: President Cross's *starting* salary was *$525,000*; he was also *awarded tenure,* although he has never taught a course in the UW or gone through the tenure process in a UW department (when I switched campuses, I had to give up tenure and start over). Put another way, by standing against faculty, *you side with people who make far more money than faculty and have far more job security.* Think about that. The man makes almost *half a million dollars more per year than me . . .* and I'm "out of touch" with the "real world"? This applies almost uniformly to Board of Regents members; does Regent Grebe make less than the average faculty member at one of the comprehensives? I'll just wager . . . no. This is a story that's not being told: almost everyone siding against faculty and these resolutions have pay and benefits that far exceed those of the targeted population. That is the definition of today's status quo. Accountability only moves downhill.

- When will the media help shift the narrative away from the lie that faculty, regardless of their feelings about the issue, have nothing at all to do with tuition? Tuition is not set by faculty, who have power over almost nothing. Yet Governor Walker and various representatives are allowed to misinform the public that current attacks on faculty, and the system, have something to do with their connection to higher tuition, which couldn't be further from the truth. There is a story here that needs to be told. That story is that we can lower tuition by increasing state support for the UW, or #fundthefreeze. That narrative shift would expose the lie that freezing tuition while simultaneously cutting the UW budget serves any purpose beyond starving the institution until it crumbles. Don't believe me? Well, the governor, who continually harps about the tuition freeze, was very much in favor of tuition increases under the public authority model; just look at his old press releases[23] (thanks Nick Fleisher): "Keeping Governor Walker's promise, the resident undergraduate tuition freeze will continue for two more years making it four straight years tuition has been frozen. After that, *the UW System Authority institutions will have flexibility to adjust tuition based on demand, making them more competitive and market-based.*" Sounds like a different tune to me, but I'm sure immature faculty are to blame somehow.

I could provide bullet points forever. *Story*: remember the legislature's outrage about the UW "cash reserves"? Those reserves have nothing to do with faculty, at all. If this was such a problem, then why has the legislature responded by moving to *increase* the power of the very administrative positions they blamed for the reserves? *Story*: faculty don't write or pass budgets or collect state revenue, yet why are they the central focus of cost "reform"? *Story*: For all the talk of "openness" and "modest" and "common sense," it wasn't modest enough to warrant public discussion. Always forgotten is the fact that these changes came via a budget bill, deliberately inserted into the process in a way to limit or eliminate discussion. *Story*: I literally have a list of fifty other items to add here.

These posts write themselves now, which is why I must move on. For some final thoughts, a few truths are worth stating clearly; these are truths that I have searched for and found. First, the no-confidence resolutions, regardless of your posi-

23. https://walker.wi.gov/newsroom/press-release/transforming -education-governor-scott-walker-announces-plan-tuition-freeze.

tion on them, have shifted points of discussion into the public in a more visible fashion. This is good. Our system president believes he has the right to conduct the business of a public university in private, and these resolutions have, by the sheer volume of discussion, helped shift the narrative. There's a long way to go. Second, faculty and staff have, throughout this process, been the truth tellers, and they've had to largely go it alone. I'm learning that that's what it takes to get a story told.

In the end, the reason this is all being made to be about faculty is to provide cover for this reality: no one wants to pay for anything anymore, ever, while still wanting the benefits provided; people who scream "taxpayer!" the loudest would rather not pay taxes (I want to pay taxes; it's one of the great acts of community). What's in store for the UW has nothing to do with resolutions, or blogs, or who said what on Tuesday. It has to do with revenue. As we all know, other people are responsible for that, many of them currently pointing their fingers at faculty members who might make 60K with a PhD for working eighty hours a week. But none of that generates revenue; policy does that. Corey Robin, in writing about similar neglect and scapegoating in the City University of New York system,[24] wrote, "Excellence doesn't come cheap. Just ask Harvard." Now that's some truth.

Thankfully, I'm done now. Beyond my subzero morale and a decade plus of people telling me I'm worthless while working my butt off and paying taxes, I'll be moving on to committee/governance work that precludes my writing much. That being said, I'm willing to turn this space over to others and a series of guest posts. Upside: you'll have nine readers, including my mom. (Hi, Mom! Love you. I'll be making sauce soon.)

24. http://coreyrobin.com/2016/05/29/the-relentless-shabbiness-of-cuny-what-is-to-be-done/.

Conclusion: Where Are We Now?

AS I WRITE THIS CONCLUSION, Donald Trump has been president of the United States for a month. Betsy DeVos, a person deeply unqualified to work in any educational field, let alone public education, has been confirmed as the secretary of education. Jerry Falwell Jr. is being considered for a task force on higher education. Immigrants, many of whom work and study in U.S. universities, are now subject to exclusion by executive order with almost no elected officials taking counteraction of any kind; we have to settle for their statements. In short, if public education was approaching a crisis state, our new national leadership, in tandem with existing state legislatures, have a clear path to cut, dismantle, and privatize. The notion that public education, and specifically higher education, might serve a purpose beyond dollars is dead. The notion that institutions can serve long-term societal goals is dead.

Ironically, back in Wisconsin, Governor Scott Walker has begun to sound reasonable by comparison. As we approach the release of the next biennial budget, Governor Walker has indicated that he wants to *increase* funding for both K–12 and the UW System, including his promise of a fully funded 5 percent tuition cut.

Does this sound too good to be true? It is.

First, any increase in funding would merely be a small offset to the massive cuts put in place by Walker himself. Second, these funding promises are attached to new "performance-based" metrics serving to enhance the purely vocational overhaul of our educational institutions as well as prioritizing short-term goals. Third, these promises primarily serve Walker's looming reelection campaign, as he seeks to distinguish himself from any intraparty challengers in the legislature who make their vocation out of demonizing public education.

And of course, there's the state legislature, who have been operating with clear intentions that show no indication of shifting. What have they accomplished in the past two years? Here is a short list:

- Another cut of $250 million to the UW System was made to deliver tax cuts.

- Tenure was eliminated. (Our system president and Board of Regents would deny this has happened, but "tenure" in the UW exists in name only. Tenure in our system has as much weight as wearing a shirt that says "tenure" on the front; it is purely symbolic.)

- Shared governance was eliminated to move to a more corporate, "advise the CEO" model. Again, our system president and Board of Regents would deny this, but they refer to governance as "shared" when arriving at desired outcomes, yet evoke executive authority when they fear the process might turn out differently.

- A new post-tenure review process was imposed that requires faculty evaluation by a single administrator with no required expertise in the relevant field of study. A simple rating of "does not meet expectations" results in remediation and possible dismissal.

- Instead of investing in our system, legislators have taken on a more pressing issue: free speech "protections" on campus. Well, not exactly. The legislature will soon codify that students can be expelled from school for the oxymoronic offense of "disruptive protests." Expensive provocateurs on speaking tours now have a right to a captive audience.

- New regents president John Behling will seek to eliminate the requirement that the UW president or chancellors have academic credentials. Enter the CEO who will "shake things up": we must have visionless managers at every level, expertise be damned.

These significant changes merely scratch the surface.

Although faculty members are routinely held responsible for the actions of administrators, we have yet another administrative scandal, with one of the UW System's former chancellors being sued for improper use of funds.[1] Given that the last administrative scandal (cash reserves) resulted in increased administrative power, this does not bode well for faculty and staff throughout the system.

Furthermore, the UW System and its campuses are routinely bullied and threatened about future funding, often in relation to minutia like the content of a specific course, a campus speaker, or demonstrations of empathy for the concerns of a minority group. One state legislator, who has ample time to micromanage the university system, has recently criticized the UW for waging a "war on men" because a campus hosts a forum for men to talk about and discuss the concept of masculinity. Examples like this are endless, as divide-and-conquer strategies are so deeply rooted and difficult to overcome. Another legislator has demanded funding be tied to the number of conservative speakers who are invited to campus events, though any attempt at "balance" would require people to turn over their voting records for verification.

1. http://www.thenorthwestern.com/story/news/2017/01/30/sonnleitner-fires-back-uw-system-lawsuit/97260478/.

As expected, the UW System is losing faculty and finds itself having to pay more than ever to keep faculty from accepting other offers. How much more? Nine million in a single semester[2] for one campus alone. This doesn't even account for the number of faculty and staff positions that have been eliminated. Sure, gutting tenure protections plays well with a fanged public, but when employees have accepted lower pay for such protections, it turns out that costs go up when the benefits are removed. We all lose as a result.

I'll end with a personal story. This year, I decided to go up for promotion to full professor, and I have already cleared all campus hurdles; only approval by the Board of Regents remains (this book will be published after they meet). Full professor is the highest rank in my profession. Way back when I was an undergraduate, I decided I wanted to go as far as I could in the area and career that I love, and I've done that. I always thought this would be momentous, that I might, even for a brief moment, receive a dose of respect from colleagues and public alike—when I published my first work as an assistant professor, I received a letter of congratulations from a local legislator. But it's been, to say the least, anticlimactic.

Why?

I almost missed my promotion hearing.

I wasn't sick or involved in some family emergency. I forgot. With tenure gone in Wisconsin, promotion feels meaningless, an accomplishment that my state, legislators, and own regents are likely to sneer at, if grudgingly accept. Even then, the promotion is even more of a rubber stamp, in that simple "program modification" can strip me of my professional life in the stroke of a pen.

2. http://archive.jsonline.com/news/education/uw-spends-nearly -9-million-in-effort-to-retain-faculty-stars-b99682882z1-371376511.html.

There are no laws, only legislators, and a partisan fever dream has replaced the Wisconsin Idea and investment in the public good.

If it hasn't already, this will be your state soon. All the fights that we thought belong to the future are owned by the present. Without that fight, without our contributions to it, and without new coalitions, the unthinkable will arrive: there will be no public education to serve as a pathway to a brighter future.

Acknowledgments

This book is dedicated to all the amazing faculty and staff of the University of Wisconsin System (we pay taxes too!). Also, thank you to anyone who took the time to read anything I wrote—our collaboration means the world to me. It is hard to say how one's thoughts and reactions in the moment will hold up over time, but the spirit of this work doubles as a promise to my daughters: I will work tirelessly to ensure that the opportunities I was privileged to have are waiting there for you when you need them. Finally, this book contains a small number of the posts that compose the entire UW Struggle series, which can be read at http://chuckrybak.com/category/uw-system.

Chuck Rybak lives in Wisconsin and is associate professor of English and humanities at the University of Wisconsin–Green Bay, where he teaches literature and creative writing. He is the author of four books of poetry, including his most recent, *</war>*.